D0534124

Children of 2010

Valora Washington and J.D. Andrews, Editors

A 1999 NAEYC Comprehensive Membership benefit

Children of 2010
Washington, D.C.

Cover illustration—Kim Lomax
Design—Melanie Rose White

Copyright © 1998 by Children of 2010 except as noted within the text. All rights reserved.

Children of 2010
1509 16th Street, N.W.
Washington, DC 20036-1426
Library of Congress Catalog Number: 98-89419
ISBN Catalog Number: 0-935989-92-7

Copies of this book are available from the National Association for the Education of Young Children. Call 202-232-8777 or 800-424-2460. Order NAEYC #390.

Printed in the United States of America.

Contents

Figures

Tables

Acknowledgments

The **Children of 2010** program wishes to recognize the contributions of dialogue participants, who gave unselfishly of their time, experience, and ideas to make this book possible. We asked them to review briefing books, attend sessions, and then reflect on the proceedings between sessions. In addition to their individual contributions, they also reached out to each other, labored to understand diverse viewpoints, and cooperated to seek a shared sense of meaning about the future needs and opportunities of children. These participants are listed on the subsequent pages of the Acknowledgments section.

The program was sponsored by the National Association for the Education of Young Children (NAEYC) and received funding from the W.K. Kellogg Foundation. In developing the concept for the **Children of 2010** program, a committee at the W.K. Kellogg Foundation provided invaluable discussions, useful advice, and programmatic support: Ann Baier, Octavia Hudson, Jean Kehoe, Rosana Rodriguez, Miguel Satut, Gerald Schmidt, Gloria Smith, and Kathy Zurcher. Additionally, Octavia Hudson, the Foundation's Communications Manager, served as a resource and a participant.

Marilyn M. Smith, Executive Director of NAEYC, was personally involved and, in addition to serving as a participant, made certain that the dialogue process had the excellent meeting, publications, and logistical support for which NAEYC is well known. Barbara Willer, Director of Public Affairs of NAEYC, contributed to planning the sessions, serving as moderator for the second and third sessions, providing suggestions about preparation of the publications, and participating in the sessions.

Dawn Vance Adams was the program's coordinator—orchestrating communications between planners, participants, and staff; arranging for meeting accommodations and a reception, recruiting and providing support for presenters, overseeing correspondence and travel support, and serving as editorial manager of documents including this book. Jim Kendrick was the principal writer for the program—developing the briefing books, writing the working papers, preparing case studies and background information, and organizing this book. Jeremy Bond assisted him as a reporter for the first two dialogue sessions.

Presenters served as catalysts for the dialogue process, and their expertise is reflected in many of the facts presented in this book. In the order of their presentations, they include Harold L. "Bud" Hodgkinson, Director of the Center for Demographic Policy; Harry P. Pachon, President of the Tomas Rivera Policy Institute; Beatriz Ceja, an Education Program Specialist for the United States Department of Education; Munier Ahmad Nazeer, a doctoral student in education policy studies and evaluation at The University of Virginia; Virginia Hodgkinson, Research Professor of Public Policy at the Center for the Study of Voluntary Organizations and Service; Jim Vance, News Anchor at WRC-NBC4 television station; Joan Lombardi, Deputy Assistant Secretary for Policy and External Affairs (ACF), U.S. Department of Health and Human Services; Barbara Harrison, News Co-Anchor at WRC-NBC4; and Geoffrey Canada, President of Rheedlen Centers for Children and Families.

Valora Washington
J.D. Andrews
Children of 2010 Co-Planners

The panel of dialogue participants

Children of 2010

Shizuko Akasaki
Los Angeles County Schools

J.D. Andrews
National Association for the
Education of Young Children

Tracey Black
Children's Television Workshop
Sesame Street Research

Barbara Bowman
Erikson Institute

Sue Bredekamp
National Association for the
Education of Young Children

Diane Camper
Annie E. Casey Foundation

Jim Carnes
Southern Poverty Law Center

Beatriz Ceja
U.S. Department of Education
Office of Migrant Programs

Richard M. Clifford
University of North Carolina-
Chapel Hill
Frank Porter Graham
Child Development Center

Dwayne Crompton
KCMC Child Development
Corporation

John Crump
National Bar Association

Jonah Martin Edelman
Stand for Children

Moe Foner
Bread and Roses Cultural Project, Inc.

Steve Fortier
CommuniTeam, Inc.

Ellen Galinsky
Families and Work Institute

Dorothy Gilliam
The Washington Post

Brian Gomes
University of Massachusetts-Amherst

Sarah Greene
National Head Start Association

Octavia Hudson
W.K. Kellogg Foundation

Jonathan J. Hutson
Center for Living Democracy

Rachel Jones
Childwire, Inc.

Sharon Lynn Kagan
Yale University Bush Center

Andrew Kennedy
Los Angeles County
Office of Education
Head Start/State Preschool

Ngoan Le
Illinois Department of Human
Services

Jim Lyons
National Association for Bilingual
Education

Barbara McCloud
Chief Leschi Schools
Sapa Dawn Center

Panel participants cont.

Munier Ahmad Nazeer
University of Virginia

Carol Brunson Phillips
Council for Early Childhood
Professional Recognition

Julian Pinkham
Yakama Tribal Court

Brigitte Rodgers
Los Angeles County Office of
Education
Head Start/State Preschool

Gloria Rodriguez
Avance

Shirley Sagawa
Learning First Alliance

Marilyn M. Smith
National Association for the
Education of Young Children

Helen Taylor
U.S. Department of Health and
Human Services
Head Start Bureau

Yasmina Vinci
National Association for Child Care
Resource and Referral Agencies

Ernest Washington
University of Massachusetts-Amherst
School of Education

Valora Washington
W.K. Kellogg Foundation

Bernice Weissbourd
Family Resource Coalition of America

Barbara Willer
National Association for the
Education of Young Children

Caroline Zinsser
Rockefeller Brothers Fund

Introduction

This book addresses some of the issues involved in making democracy work for the next generation of children, who we call *the children of 2010*. It is based on a series of dialogues conducted in 1998 by a small group of national leaders who are involved in creating a better future for children, youth and their families. Rather than serve as a meeting report, however, the book seeks to challenge readers to pursue their own exploration of ideas and actions that will contribute to an inclusive democracy for all of our children.

A stimulus for the **Children of 2010** initiative is the increasing demographic diversity of children in the United States. Los Angeles alone has over 100 ethnic groups who speak 70 languages. Elsewhere, our small towns and suburbs, as well as the great cities, are becoming home to a larger proportion of U.S.-born people of color and immigrants. By 2010, children of color will represent the majority of young people in California, Florida, New York, and Texas—the states that will account for a third of the nation's youth. By the middle of the 21st century, demographers forecast that Americans of color will represent a majority of the overall U.S. population.

People of color is a broad term applied to a diversity of racial and ethnic groups who are not non-Hispanic European Whites. This includes individuals of African, Latino/Hispanic, Asian-Pacific Islander, and Native American descent. Within racial and ethnic groups, of course, are many other distinctions, such as Chinese, Korean, and Indonesian. In addition, an increasing number of children have parents from more than one racial or ethnic group.

What is unique about the 21st century is that, eventually, no single racial or ethnic group will constitute a majority of the U.S. population. This means that democracy will require an unprecedented level of cooperation, communication, and teamwork among people who are different.

Dialogue and democracy require hard work

The dialogue sessions for **Children of 2010** were demanding and sometimes difficult. The participants were intentionally diverse—representing a broad range of professions, ages, racial and ethnic groups, organizations, and viewpoints. Sometimes we did not agree with each other. Simply communicating clearly among ourselves could be exhausting.

"Dialogue" is a method of group exploration and discovery, and we embraced this approach because of our belief that a balanced and achievable vision of the future requires a group effort that is as inclusive as possible. All of us, in a democracy, own the future; and we must all help define it. The word *dialogue* comes from two Greek roots that produce the concept of creating "meaning with each other." The word *discussion* on the other hand stems from the Latin word, *discutere,* which means "to smash to pieces." So, while *discussion* is a conversational form that often produces fragmentation, *dialogue,* with its emphasis on collective meaning, leads to mutual respect and building the capacity to work together.

Because the sessions were an exploratory first step, the participants did not have a "road map." We were often unsure where the discussions would lead, and often we would complete a day of dialogue without a sense of closure. There were so many loose ends and unresolved issues!

In retrospect, the difficulty of the process—which sometimes generated a sense of frustration—was a necessary ingredient for the visioning process. It challenged our complacency and the easy answers. We were forced to question, explore, reflect, think of new solutions, and grow as human beings.

In a sense, the dialogue process is a microcosm of democracy. There is disagreement, conflict, compromise, communication, competition, and debate. It is the crucible in which participatory change occurs.

It is our desire that this book

be equally challenging, and even disquieting, to readers. If it achieves its goal, it will raise questions and troubling issues. Hopefully, it will challenge you to become dissatisfied with the status quo—prompting you to reach out in search of a better future for the children of 2010. The next generation will access the 21st century democracy they deserve only if we learn from each other, change, become energized, and move forward.

What is democracy, anyway?

It is important for every generation to examine its vision because democracy is a journey, not a static condition. Conditions change, and the vision grows.

Rather than seek to define democracy too precisely, which is admittedly subject to a variety of definitions and debate, we simply wish to point out that democracy in the United States has evolved. It will continue to do so.

Initially, the U.S. vision of democracy was much narrower than it is today. Even towering founders like Thomas Jefferson, who inspired movements toward democracy around the world, could not envision a society where their bold ideas would apply to women, slaves, or Native Americans. The broadening of political democracy would require many decades of social change—a process that continues today.

But the United States has applied the idea of democracy to community services as well as to the ballot box. To illustrate, the idea of a universal public education for all children spread slowly among the States during the 19th century. Throughout the 20th century, the nation has struggled with how to apply tax-supported education fairly, as evidenced by court decisions and legislation addressing such issues as civil rights and the needs of children with disabilities.

The idea of democracy has been applied to the economy as well. After World War II, for example, a grateful nation granted a "GI Bill" for millions of youthful veterans so they could have an opportunity to attend college, own a home, access medical care, and gain preferential treatment in government employment.

Our vision

All of our children must have fair access to the nurturing and preparation necessary for full participation in our democracy. This encompasses social, economic, political, and cultural participation. It also involves the competencies and experience needed to be active, involved, and responsible citizens.

We believe that each child is a national treasure. Each has unique personality traits, heritage, and abilities that our society needs. Each can—and must—be a vital participant in 21st century democracy. Each must be respected for his or her uniqueness, and each must also have the preparation to succeed in the larger, heterogeneous society that is becoming increasingly global and technological in its orientation.

In the past and present, some children have not been treasured by society nor given access to the opportunities they need to develop as full participants in a democracy. There are many barriers. Among these are prejudice: racism, sexism, classism, antagonism toward languages other than English, cultural chauvinism, and religious bigotry. Community institutions have erected barriers when they are ineffective in responding to the individuality of children, such as their learning styles, developmental differences, and disabilities. Tragically for some children, there are even barriers to survivability: violence, lack of access to health care, malnutrition, and accidents.

Yet, we have hope that barriers such as these are surmountable. The miracle of the United States is that it can and does change—often for the better! The milestones of change are far too numerous to recount here. They include the Bill of Rights, the abolition movement, women's suffrage, child labor laws, the safe food and drug laws, environmental protection, and equal employment opportunity.

With ample grounds for hope, we therefore believe that it is possible to achieve the social change necessary to give all of our children fair and equitable access to the preparation necessary for full participation in a democracy that encompasses everyone. Our vision is grounded in the tradition of Abraham Lincoln and Martin Luther King. Together, our children can be one nation, moving toward the realization of e pluribus unum—one nation out of many peoples.

Incentives for social change

There are quite a few doomsayers in our midst. Some public commentators speculate that the increasing diversity of the U.S. population will lead to heightened tensions and race wars. Some speak of the breakdown of the nation into the *haves* and the *have-nots*. The *haves* will enjoy access to nurturing, quality education and advancement, knowledge work, and unprecedented affluence. The *have nots* will be relegated to deteriorating neighborhoods, inferior schools, scant opportunities, menial minimum-wage jobs, and hopelessness.

The pronouncements of the doomsayers have a certain value, because their words should shock us into an unrelenting determination to create a much better future for our children. In *A Christmas Carol*, the ghosts of Christmas gave Scrooge a chance to view the consequences of his stubbornly cold heart. He had a chance to change, and so do we.

Democracy has a price, and a nation that fails to pay will lose it.

Democracy relies on an informed and involved citizenry, requiring the preparation and competency of all of its children. The democratic paradigm expects participation, volunteerism, and community problem solving. For example, community schools and early childhood programs depend on volunteers, parent participation in decisionmaking, and unpaid leaders. As they become adults, the children of 2010 must be prepared to join with diverse neighbors in filling these roles.

Increasingly, our democracy will rely on citizens who can work, communicate, and share power with fellow Americans who are different. Community institutions and businesses will serve "customers" who are culturally diverse. And economic participation in our democracy requires unprecedented levels of skills, knowledge and productivity.

Description of the dialogue sessions

The National Association for the Education of Young Children sponsored a series of three dialogue sessions in Washington, D.C., during 1998. These activities were supported with funds from the W.K. Kellogg Foundation. The overall theme was the **Children of 2010.** The first meeting in April focused on "Exploring the Knowledge Base," encompassing projections of demographics and the barriers that young people—and their parents—face when attempting to gain fair access to resources for education and personal development. The second dialogue in May addressed "Best Practices," seeking to identify the underlying principles and attributes of promising child development programs. The third session in August moved toward establishing a vision for the children of 2010.

The sessions were intentionally spread out over a number of months to allow time for reflection, because "facts" were just the beginning of the dialogue process. Many participants found it necessary to challenge their pet assumptions and strategies for change. The world of 2010 will be different from the experiences and paradigms of the 1980s or 1960s, and we had to take time to learn, grow, and find a fresh vision that would be appropriate to the next century.

Presenters for the sessions were selected on the basis of their ability to present vital facts and provoke our thinking. Much of the time at the meetings was reserved for interactions among participants.

Before each session, a briefing book was distributed to participants, consisting of fact sheets, recent articles, excerpts from books, and even poetry. After each session, a working paper was prepared to capture the key ideas, facts, and topics.

This book is an edited compilation of materials from both the briefing books and working papers. We have organized the materials by topic, without making any distinction regarding whether they originally appeared in the briefing books or working papers. Some of the copyrighted articles and book excerpts have not been included here because of the lengthy process of obtaining permissions for large-scale reproduction.

We have structured each section of the book into four parts: focusing, exploring, reflecting, and dialoging. This reflects the dialogue process:

Focusing on a theme

Exploring information

Reflecting on what we have learned

Dialoging the facts and our thoughts with others to expand the ideas.

We need you

Throughout the dialogue sessions, participants reiterated their desire to involve many more people and to take the dialogues "home" to their communities and other spheres of influence. This book is intended as a next step toward broadening the process of exploring and visioning democracy in the next century—and creating a society where all of our children have fair access to the American dream.

The 1998 dialogues in Washington, D.C., were only a start. There were many topics and issues that we could not address because of time limitations. Integrating age-specific issues into a developmental continuum for children from prebirth through age 18 (or older) was not addressed. Urgent community-specific topics were not on the agenda. The role of parents and how to involve them in creating a better future for the children of 2010 needed much more attention. How to break down the walls between programs, agencies and professions—to achieve a unified effort to advance the wellbeing of our children and youth—awaits your consideration as well.

Dialogue is an exploratory process. Through group participation, it seeks to form a vision and identify those issues that may affect efforts to realize that vision. Dialogue is not intended as highly structured research. Many of the observations and comments in this book should be viewed as hypotheses supported by credible information, rather than "research conclusions." The dialogue sessions do, however, suggest many areas where additional primary and secondary research would be helpful.

Suggestions about how to use this book

We hope that you will read this book as part of a group and use it to launch your own dialogues about how to build a better future for the children of 2010 in your community, your workplace, and your profession. The book alone will spark some ideas, but engaging in group discussion can multiply the impact.

If at all possible, include people who are different within your dialogue group. Examples would be professionals, parents, and youth; people of different races and ethnic groups; young adults, baby boomers, and senior citizens; professionals from different disciplines or workplaces. The different perspectives will enrich your exploration and visioning process.

At the conclusion of each section, the book suggests discussion topics. Use these—or your own questions—to spark further exploration and discovery.

In addition to reading and talking about this book, there are four ways that you can use the focus on children of 2010:

Adapt it. Adapt the exploration process to the specific characteristics and needs within your community or workplace.

Act on it. Making a better future for the next generation of children requires action. After you explore and discuss, identify an issue or topic for action. Get other people involved and make your community a better place!

Extend it. There are many important topics that were beyond the scope of our brief dialogue sessions. You will contribute to the visioning process by addressing additional issues and sharing your explorations with all of us.

Integrate it. Developing children and youth involves so many variables! How do we connect the issues? You can contribute to a better future for the next generation through fresh thinking that integrates these issues into better strategies and more effective action.

We appreciate the work performed by the participants at our dialogue sessions, and we look forward to your contribution to building a democracy that nurtures and treasures all of the children of 2010.

Democracy for a New Century

Focusing

One nation, indivisible?

Focusing on the children of 2010 is an important step in preparing ourselves, other adults, and our children for a future country where people are quite different from one another in terms of culture, race, and language. Being able to live, work, learn, and prosper together—in the context of these differences—will be a matter of economic, social, and political necessity because the only majority in the 21st century is a rainbow.

In the year 2010, the number of children of immigrants will rise to 9 million, representing over one-fifth of the school-age population. Four states—California, Florida, New York, and Texas—will account for a third of the nation's youth, and a majority of these young people will be ethnic minorities.[1] The wave of change will continue to broaden after 2010, and this diverse mosaic of perspectives has the potential for conflict—both between ethnic groups and with the 76 million baby boomers who reach age 65.

A "happy ending" for the drama confronting our children and youth is by no means certain, and some commentators have predicted the disintegration of community and shared purpose into a Disunited States. However, we are convinced that thoughtful and committed Americans can, once again, grapple successfully with the historic challenge of reinventing democracy and moving constructively toward the ideal of "one nation, indivisible. . . ."

It is imperative that everyone explore the implications of the new diversity and how we, as a society, can set a course toward constructive and inclusive outcomes that will benefit everyone. Rather than abandon the next 12 years to chance or the risk of negative outcomes, we owe it to our chil-

9

dren to look thoughtfully at the future, explore the facts, identify solutions that work, and outline a vision of how they will indeed be a *United* States.

Neither the dialogues conducted during 1998 nor this book about the children of 2010 have "solved" the identifiable problems. The coming changes affect everyone, and all must be part of the solution. Yet what **Children of 2010** can accomplish is important. Participants of the dialogues—and discussion groups that you, the book readers form—can frame the initial issues, identify promising solutions, and outline an action strategy for engaging the nation in a process of preparation. You can also implement needed change in your community, statehouse, profession, and workplace. While there is still time.

Exploring
Demographic eye-openers

We all make assumptions about "what other people are like," and these notions are not always grounded in reality. In preparing for dialogue, we committed ourselves to review the facts. The Director of the Center for Demographic Policy, Dr. Harold Hodgkinson,[2] challenged us all to take a clearer look at population characteristics—both for today and for the future. The following are statistics gathered by Hodgkinson to highlight trends:

Worldwide

Of the 5.7 billion people on the planet, only 17 percent are White, dropping to 9 percent by 2010.

Most young girls in the *world* will have to combine making a living with raising children.

Many other nations have higher rates of unmarried births than the United States—50 percent in Sweden and 33 percent in France, compared to 30 percent in the United States.

United States

Half of all people in the United States live in suburbs, a quarter in core cities, and a quarter in small towns/rural areas.

Only a quarter of U.S. households consist of a married couple with one or more children at home.

A quarter of households consist of people living alone.

An eighth of households are single mothers with children.

There are now over 56,000 people in the United States who are over 100 years of age, and the *third* quarter of human life is now age 50 to 75.

The greatest increase in poor families since 1990 has occurred in close-in suburbs, not in core cities.

Between 1970 and the early 1990s, the poverty rate increases were greater for Whites (38%) than for African Americans (19%).

Mothers (U.S.)

Over 70 percent of school-age children have working mothers.

Most unmarried and teen mothers are White; higher *percentages* are African American and Hispanic.

Children

Children under 6 are more likely to be poor than any other age group of Americans.

In 1950, 40 percent of the poor were elderly and 10 percent were children; but in 1990, 40 percent of the poor were children and 10 percent were elderly.

Over 20 percent of U.S. children are being raised below the poverty line, the highest percentage of all NATO nations.

Sixty-two percent of poor young children live with at least one parent/relative who works (1994). Only 28 percent of poor young children lived with parents on welfare.

Between 1970 and the early 1990s, young-child poverty increased faster in the suburbs (59%) than cities (34%).

Transiency

43 million Americans move every year, more than any other nation.

Transiency is the greatest enemy of family stability, school dropouts, and a major predictor of high crime rates.

Where do parents fit into the picture?

One of the persistent questions in the dialogue sessions was, Where do parents fit into the picture? Parents, after all, are instrumental in child development and a large constituency for positive change. In addition to providing time, money, and commitment, they are the "glue" that binds together the overall developmental process from prebirth to adulthood. However, for parents to ensure that all children of 2010 have a fair start in life, they must have access to resources and an empowering role. Subject to further deliberation, some of these may include

- A right and responsibility to play a central role in their children's education and development

- Enough money so the family can live in decency and stability
- Access to health care for their children, and jobs with reasonable health care benefits
- Quality public services for tax dollars expended, regardless of neighborhood or economic status
- Schools that produce positive results for all children
- Community and institutional support for the goal that each child can develop his or her potential to participate fully and successfully in the U.S. economy and democracy
- Respect by community institutions for each parent's culture and values
- Access to a safe home and neighborhood where the family can live
- Positive, affirming recreational and social activities for young people
- Access to appropriate child care for working parents
- Support through religious organizations or other means for nurturing in their children the parents' sense of values and moral commitments
- Media and cultural messages that reaffirm positive values and goals
- Reasonable accommodation by employers to parental responsibilities
- Access to affordable postsecondary education and training for their children

Money matters

The resources that children need are beyond the financial reach of many parents. Indeed, a low family income is one of the greatest challenges to the well-being of the children of 2010. There has been a dramatic expansion of wealth in the United States during the past two decades, but the gains are concentrated among the top 20% of U.S. households. Households in the bottom 40% of households actually *lost* wealth.

Between 1983 and 1989, the rich got richer, and the poor became poorer, according to Dr. Virginia Hodgkinson, a research professor at Georgetown Public Policy Institute. When households are divided into five groups (quintiles), the *top* one-fifth gained 96% of increases in real wealth between 1983 and 1989. The *lower middle* quintile lost 1% in terms of real wealth, and the *bottom* lost 9%. Figure 1 depicts this disparity, using data from a book by Edward N. Wolff.[3]

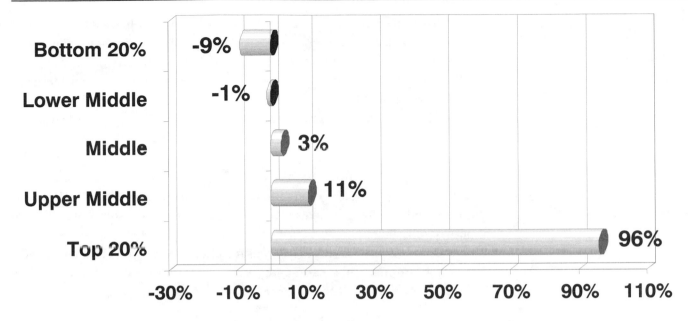

Figure 1. Change in real wealth distribution by income quintile, 1983–1989

While the very wealthy generally have above-average household incomes, much of their wealth is in the form of "net worth." The wealthiest 1% of households possess nearly half (48%) of all net financial assets. In all, one out of 10 households (10%) possess over 83% of net financial assets, as well as over 72% of total, overall net worth. In 1989, 3.4 million wealth holders had a net worth of $4.8 trillion.

The presentation by Virginia Hodgkinson included a discussion about *wealth*fare: The U.S. government spends 350% in welfare for the rich as it does for the poor, she said, citing Zepezauer and Naiman.[4] Among the federal wealthfare spending cited were

Table 1
"Wealthfare" spending

Military waste and fraud	$172 Billion
Social Security tax inequities	$53 Billion
Accelerated depreciation	$37 Billion
Savings and loan bailout	$32 Billion
Tax avoidance by transnationals	$12 Billion
Lower taxes on capital gains	$37 Billion

Contra Costa Child Care Council
Learning Institute
1035 Detroit Ave. Suite 200
Concord, CA 94518

In capping Social Security taxes at $62,700, families making the median U.S. income pay 7.65% of payroll income, but individuals making 10 times as much are charged only 1.46% of their payroll income. Moreover, 97% of the benefit of reduced capital gains taxes goes to the wealthiest 1%. In balancing the budget by 2002, the federal government is cutting the social welfare programs 10 times more than financial assistance for the wealthy.

According to Hodgkinson, public policy regarding the federal budget and taxation have been steadily shifting in favor of the wealthy. In 1950, the total taxes paid by corporations were 31%, but the total has dropped to 11% in 1997. Taxes on wealthy individuals have been cut by 50% since 1977. She questioned whether this was a real or equitable partnership among members of our society.

Certainly the resources for health care, schools, postsecondary education, job training, child care, and positive activities for children and youth are extremely difficult to access if millions of parents are losing wealth.

Race and "one America"

E pluribus unum, one out of many, is the national motto. Yet, the children of 2010 will be tested when they apply this ideal to a society that is becoming increasingly diverse. In a nation where no single race or culture will ultimately be in the majority, the next generation will be called upon to work together—to move beyond the injustice, intolerance, resentment, and anger that has been such weighty baggage in U.S. history.

Making democracy work in a 21st century society that is characterized by tolerance, cooperation, and diversity will require change. Some people are unaware of what constitutes an inclusive society. One of the meeting's leaders recalled what happened when, as a Black woman, she moved into a White neighborhood in Michigan. Her neighbors now assumed that one African-American resident made their neighborhood inclusive.

Minorities also have divergent impressions of racial issues. A study cited by one participant compared perception of prejudice with educational level. Those with less education didn't think there was as much prejudice as minorities who had reached higher educational levels. This suggests that empowering minorities educationally will allow everyone to better understand how racism affects them. That better understanding allows everyone to see the realities: for example, that White high-school graduates earn more than African-American graduates do.

To really understand diversity issues, the dialogue group looked beyond the numbers (one participant complained that minorities are usually considered in terms of numbers.) The group looked for attitudes. What attitudes are fostering separation or exclusion, and how will our children move beyond them?

First, the numbers. The number of incarcerated young Black men has skyrocketed; one-third of Black men between the ages of 18 and 34 are either in jail, on parole or previously in jail. A fact like this, though caused by multiple factors, contributes to resentment of injustice by African Americans and negative stereotyping by Whites.

Second, prejudice and racism still touch the lives of minorities every day. One university-based participant cited administrators who were former members of the Ku Klux Klan. The most pernicious attitudes, though, were more subtle. The most common expressions of racism, one person said, were the more mundane, everyday things. The fact that Black men can't get a taxi, for instance.

Third, people tend to relate what they see to themselves. The panel was shown a *Time* magazine cover[5] that featured a computer-engineered face of a woman. The computer combined people of many different races and ethnic backgrounds to create the woman. The panel was told the origin

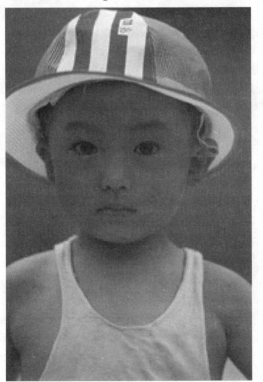

of the woman, but previous studies revealed that the woman was seen as the race of the observer. Whites saw a White woman. Blacks saw a Black woman. Asians saw an Asian woman. A future population accustomed to diversity might see her as she was: a part of everyone. Or see her as an individual, who doesn't need to be "categorized."

The discussion also emphasized that diversity continues to expand in many dimensions. More grandparents serve as parents. Children are being raised by gay and lesbian parents. The group agreed: We must work in the context of each child.

So how can we help our children develop a more successfully diverse society? We need to develop certain values, said one participant. Values that build a completely multiethnic, multiracial society. Values that would apply to everyone, in every country.

"Can we make an idea bigger than itself?" one of the meeting leaders challenged the group. "To come out of an atmosphere of disrespect? . . . I believe this is possible because I've seen it happen." She grew up taking daylong family car trips, complete with meals, because her parents could not stop anywhere since only Whites had access to public accommodations. Now, her daughter has full access to restaurants, hotels, public transportation, movie theaters, rest rooms, and water fountains—all unthinkable only 35 years ago in certain parts of the country. E pluribus unum is a possible dream.

Hope

"There is hope" about relations between different racial and ethnic groups in an increasingly diverse nation. Despite injustices and brutal incidents, constructive changes have occurred in recent U.S. history. A case in point is school desegregation. Within our lifetime, the majority of Whites in the United States have moved from viewing segregation as "the way of life" in the South to being shocked that Americans and their institutions could have ever sanctioned these outrageous practices.

Today's children are shocked by the real-life story of Ruby Bridges, a 6-year-old African American girl who withstood angry White mobs, tomatoes, spit, and epithets to integrate the New Orleans schools in 1960. White parents withdrew their children from Ruby's class, leaving her as the sole student in the classroom for a year. Now, some White students identify with Ruby and the other African Americans, rather than the White segregationists.

Accountability for additional change

The dialogue participants acknowledged that there needs to be a great deal of additional change to prepare our communities and nation for the children of 2010, and the youth who participated in the dialogue sessions challenged the group to be accountable for additional change. "Make a list of the changes that need to occur," one said. "When I have your job in 2010, check off what you have accomplished, and I'll go on from there."

One of the meeting planners also challenged the group to take a fresh look at the injustices that our children will face unless we take appropriate actions now. "I do not want to be in a position of having to explain, to the next generation, some of the horror stories that persist in our communities," she said. "I do not want to explain why some children cannot go to the doctor. I do not want to explain why our educational system provides an unequal education to people of color. I do not want to explain why our society imprisons so many young Black men."

Change is necessary at all levels—from national policy to individual behavior. Some may require improvements in programs for children and families, but others are a matter of much broader action. One participant noted, for example, that a child's self image—and vision of who he or she can become—are shaped in part by the reactions of others, including neighbors and teachers who may be intolerant.

New tools for social change

Another participant, an organization development and youth program specialist, challenged the panel to find new tools—such as community dialogues—for achieving social change. The emergence of a multicultural society challenges us to enlarge our toolkit for achieving positive social change. Fortunately, a variety of theories and methods have evolved, and these are already being implemented with encouraging results in a variety of communities and organizations.

Historically, social change has tended to be specific to an issue, such as child labor laws or equal access to public accommodations, or to specific populations, such as women who pressed for voting rights or factory workers who organized labor unions. In the increasingly multicultural and complex society of today, we often need additional tools to address change in the context of diverse populations, multiple issues, and whole systems of interrelated actions.

A book by Marvin Weisbord, *Discovering Common Ground,*[6] reviews the lineage of change strategies over the past hundred years. While elements of earlier change strategies continue to be employed, there has been a fundamental shift in approach. In the early 1900s, we looked to individuals—experts, reformers, issues people, and muckraking journalists—to lead the assault on social problems. Today, promising new methods in our toolkit focus on community and organizational participation, where everybody is actively involved in improving (i.e., changing) the system.

The trend toward broad, cross-sectional participation was identifiable by the 1950s, when a wide range of stakeholders became direct participants in solving community and organizational problems. Some of the early efforts were disappointing, because solutions tended to be piecemeal. By the mid-1960s, however, systems theory—which seeks to identify the relationships between whole constellations of resources, processes, outputs, and outcomes—became widely accepted. Broadened participation was married to systems concepts, and problem-solving became more capable of addressing complex, persistent, long-term issues. Eventually, this trend became all-inclusive so that, today, there are "learning organizations" and "learning communities," in which all stakeholders, resources, and processes become an organism that is collectively capable of continuous change (and improvement).

We have gained many rights and freedoms, and today's economic vitality is providing opportunities for many, though not all, people in America. Yet, most would agree that we as a nation are falling short of our goals for health, education, safe communities, equal access to economic empowerment, and race relations. In just the past decade, new methods for involving a wide range of people in problem-solving, system-wide planning, and visioning have emerged. Open Space Technology, Future Search Conferences, and Dialogues are new and emerging processes that are having a significant impact on the effectiveness of social change efforts in the 1990s.

In Oakland, California; Kansas City, Missouri; and Racine, Wisconsin, literally thousands of citizens are coming together to create a shared vision and systemic plan of action to create healthy, thriving, and safe communities.[7] Organizations such as the U.S. Department of Health and Human Services and Seattle's Pathfinder Elementary School are employing methods of inclusion to create the systems that allow them to be more effective. These are but a few examples of the changing face of methods for achieving positive change. The methods are enabling people to create the social bonds, as well as the plans of action, that allow them to reach for their shared vision and implement it. Undoubtedly, we will continue to learn from these new approaches, making use of the tactics that work and improving on those that don't. Given that many of the new approaches to social change tap into and unleash the passion, concern, experience, and insights of many more people than the change processes of the past, one thing is certain: It is a much more exciting time for the millions of Americans who want to make a difference in the systems which affect them. And it is a model for change that can accommodate a society of diversity, where it is imperative that we come together, inclusively, to change the systems which hold our social problems in place.

Reflecting

The briefing books included cultural material and news articles as a means for opening up our minds to discussion, viewpoints and feelings of others, and new ideas. We are sharing samples of these items in this book.

Johnny Thomas
by Sterling A. Brown

Dey sent John Thomas
To a one-room school;
Teacher threw him out
For a consarned fool.

His pappy got drunk,—
Beat de boy good,
Lashed his back
Till it sprouted blood.

He took up gamblin',
Took up pool,
A better business that
For a consarned fool.

He got a 'fancy woman'
Took his every dime,
Kept Johnny gamblin'
All de time

De jack run low
De gal run out
Johnny didn't know
What 'twas all about.

Asked de fancy woman
"Come on back,"
Fancy woman tell him,
"Git de Jack."

Johnny was a tadpole,
Sheriff was an eel,
Caught him jes' as soon
As he started to steal.

Put him on de chain gang,
Handled him cruel,
Jes' de sort of treatment
For a consarned fool.

Guard lashed Johnny
An awful lick,
Johnny split his head
Wid a muddy pick.

Dey haltered Johnny Thomas
Like a cussed mule,
Dey hung Johnny Thomas
For a consarned fool.
Dropped him in de hole
Threw de slack lime on,
Oughta had mo' sense
Dan to evah git born.

How the World Will Judge Us

. . . if we cannot fulfill our own ideals here, we cannot expect others to accept them. And when the youngest child alive today has grown to the cares of manhood, our position in the world will be determined first of all by what provisions we make today—for his education, his health, and his opportunities for a good home and a good job and a good life.

—John F. Kennedy, 1962 State of the Union Address

Surely Not Good Enough

It surely is not enough for the most powerful nation in the world to have an educational system that is impoverished not only in terms of its dilapidated physical facilities but also in terms of inequities along racial and class lines among schools and school districts. I hope that you will agree that it is not enough for us to move at a snail's pace in wiping out the remnants of racial and ethnic strife. In doing so, we merely add to the burdens we must bear in leading the world toward a lasting peace, devoid of the sentiments and enmities that have already brought on huge wars time and again. We can do better than that, and I hope that you agree.

—John Hope Franklin,
speaking before the North Carolina General Assembly, July 22, 1997

The Next Wave
How Immigration Blurs The Race Discussion
by Roberto Suro

In a 1970 essay entitled "What America Would Be Like Without Blacks," Ralph Ellison evoked the image of European immigrants learning the epithet "nigger" as soon as they got off the boat because "it made them feel instantly American." Blacks, Ellison argued, served as "a marker, a symbol of limits, a metaphor for the outsider," and so Whites, even the most recently arrived and poorest immigrants, "could look at the social position of Blacks and feel that color formed an easy and reliable gauge of determining to what extent one was or was not an American."

Today, we are again living through a new era of immigration and must ask once more what role the color line plays in the process of becoming American. European immigrants suffered ugly, sometimes violent, bias but their offspring have acquired all the status and privilege that goes along with being white-skinned. Indeed, during some of the desegregation battles of the 1960s and 1970s, White "ethnics" rejected Blacks just as bitterly as the old stock Anglo-Saxons of the South.

Now the question is whether Latino and Asian newcomers and their offspring will end up on the "white" side of the color line, thus disastrously hardening the exclusion of Blacks, or on the "black" side, meaning that they could be excluded too. I hold hope for another possibility: This wave of immigration might spark a process of social change that blurs, perhaps even erases, the sharp division between black and white that has scarred the nation's soul since its founding.

The question of whether the new immigrants will be treated as white, black or something else is transforming the way Americans are talking about race. The change became evident to me when I joined seven other panelists and moderator Jim Lehrer of the "NewsHour" for a conversation on race with President Clinton that was broadcast on PBS July 9—the third and final such event in the president's year-long race initiative.

Thirty years ago, the issues would have been sharply defined. For example, everyone would have known exactly what "desegregation" meant and probably would have espoused strong views. But during this discussion, whether the topic was the nature of discrimination or the appropriate limits to affirmative action, we all had problems finding the right terms for the questions, let alone the answers. Clinton seized on this dilemma when he said that "we need a vocabulary that embraces America's future, and we need a vocabulary that embraces America's present and past on this race issue."

Our current vocabulary of race is inadequate because it describes a world seen only in black and white. The problem is not simply that we have added new groups to the mix. The language of black/white differences is losing its meaning because Latinos and Asians do not fit into a world in which people are permanently and definitively marked either as insiders or outsiders.

Elaine Chao of the Heritage Foundation made that point near the start of the "NewsHour" special when she spoke of Chinese Americans in San Francisco who have suffered explicit prejudice as a minority group, but who now sometimes are counted as white. She gave the example of a boy denied admission to a desirable public school because Chinese Americans were already "over-represented" among the high achievers. Chao said this was a case of "unfair treatment based on race." It might be a case of reverse discrimination, but that term was coined for whites who claimed victimization by programs designed to benefit minorities and I'm not sure if it makes sense in this context.

What do you call people who were once the victims of racism but have crossed over into the realm of relative privilege, as measured by academic and economic achievement? You can't call them "white," even in symbolic terms if you are talking about Asian Americans. Despite their successes, they still suffer real discrimination on many fronts and are still viewed as outsiders by many of their fellow Americans—black, white and Latino.

This role of crossing back and forth across the seemingly insuperable color line in American society is not new to Latinos or Asians. In South Texas, for example, Jim Crow segregation applied to blacks in the 1940s while Mexican Americans suffered a less institutionalized but equally vicious form of discrimination. When Latinos emulated blacks and brought civil rights cases under the Equal Protection Clause of the Fourteenth Amendment, the Texas courts ruled that Latinos were technically white. Since the Fourteenth Amendment was a post-Civil War remedy, the courts ruled that it only recognized two groups needing to be treated equally—blacks and whites. So Latinos could not claim any relief.

In 1954, Mexican-American civil rights lawyers got to the U.S. Supreme Court with a case, Hernandez v. Texas, in which they showed that no person of Mexican descent had sat on a jury in Jackson County for 25 years. According to Texas practice, it was okay to bring Pete Hernandez and all other Latino defendants before all-white juries because it was just whites judging whites. Writing for a unanimous court, Chief Justice Earl Warren noted that in the Jackson County courthouse, Latinos were obliged to use the restrooms marked "colored," that their children attended segregated schools and that at least one restaurant in town prominently displayed a sign announcing "No Mexicans Served."

All of this, the court decided, was ample proof that Mexican Americans constituted "a separate class in Jackson County, distinct from 'whites.'" The civil rights struggle that sprang from that decision and other similar rulings is now mature. Just in the past few years, federal courts in California, Texas and Florida have found in major voting rights cases that Latinos were denied fair political representation. Given the freshness of this history, it seems unlikely that Latinos can simply be regarded as white as a matter of legal status anytime soon. But their place on the color line is fuzzier when it comes to social and economic status.

Shortly before the 1996 death of former Texas congresswoman and black civil rights leader Barbara Jordan, she proposed drastic cuts in the number of low-skilled legal immigrants allowed into the country in order to remedy the plight of poor Americans who might otherwise find work in urban labor markets. Implicit in the proposal put forth by the U.S. Commission on Immigration Reform, which Jordan then headed, was the notion that employers, overwhelmingly white, preferred to hire low-skilled immigrants, overwhelmingly Latino, over the native poor, especially blacks.

"The fact of the matter is that white people feel more comfortable around Hispanics than they do around blacks," said Danny Bakewell, president of the Brotherhood Crusade Black United Front, a Los Angeles economic development group. He was explaining the failure of a program to get young blacks hired in hotel catering jobs in the aftermath of the 1992 Rodney King riots. Similar views are shared by many African Americans who complain that Latino immigrants are often favored in the workplace. Social scientists have not been able to determine conclusively whether such displacement exists, but on such matters perceptions can be as important as facts. There is little doubt blacks increasingly see Latinos as competitors for jobs, neighborhood control and political influence.

The ambiguous position of Latinos and Asians who straddle the racial divide today almost seems to have been forecast in the Hernandez decision more than half a century ago. "Throughout our history differences in race and color have defined easily identifiable groups which have at times required the aid of the courts in securing equal treatment under the laws," Warren wrote. "But community prejudices are not static, and from time to time other differences from the community norm may define other groups which need the same protection."

This extraordinary but nearly forgotten ruling can still instruct us. The black experience in American history has a unique and permanent importance that must always inform civil rights policies, but guaranteeing equality requires a recognition of the dynamism in American society, including the dynamism of prejudice. Warren's understanding of bias is all the more important today because of the demographic and economic changes that the nation is undergoing.

The groups that do not fit the old racial paradigms—Asians and Latinos—are growing rapidly due to immigration and high birth rates, while blacks and whites are not. Moreover, all racial and ethnic groups are now segmented according to economic status, if not in the same proportions. In other words, being white is no longer a clear sign of being in the majority and enjoying privileged status. Whites are on the way to becoming a numerical minority in several cities. Meanwhile, several nationalities of Asian immigrants, Indians and Filipinos for example, have higher levels of education and higher earnings than whites, on average. And there is a surging Latino middle class across the nation. Moreover, being black is no longer a certain marker of outsider status given the economic and political gains achieved by African Americans over the past 30 years. And some Asian nationalities, Cambodians and Laotians, along with the largest Latino immigrant nationalities, Mexicans, Salvadorans and Dominicans, suffer higher overall poverty rates than blacks.

Bias, too, has become more complex than when skin color was enough to determine admission to a public institution. Racism persists, and it may even be widespread, but it persists primarily as a privately held belief, rather than as public behavior that is socially acceptable, let alone legally sanctioned.

However, group differences in educational and economic status persist with whites enjoying overall advantages despite the fact that overt institutional prejudice has largely been dismantled. This fact points to structural barriers buried deep in our schools and labor market that restrict opportunity and foment intergenerational poverty.

Not surprisingly then, almost every conversation about race these days verges on a discussion of class. It happened repeatedly during the "NewsHour" special and Clinton even suggested that economic status can serve as a proxy for race. "I think the point I wanted to make," the president said, "is to whatever extent you can have an economic approach that embraces people of all races, if it elevates disproportionately racial groups that have been disproportionately depressed, you'll help to deal with the race problem."

Latino and Asian immigration drives home the realization that there are still harsh dividing lines in American society today but that these lines are not solely based on color. A person's race cannot be changed, but the quality of their education and their economic prospects can be. That means society can attempt both to dismantle barriers and to help the disadvantaged cross them if it so chooses. The sheer demographic weight of immigration will oblige Americans to address these challenges in the future. History teaches that such challenges are resolved through a process that includes conflict and competition, but that in the end, the nation emerges stronger for it.

That is why I believe we will develop a new vocabulary of race to describe a future that is now taking shape. As Clinton suggested, this new vocabulary must embrace history, especially the black experience in America. And if it does, we may yet build a more perfect union and redeem our painful past.

©1998 The Washington Post. Reprinted with permission.

[Statistical charts published with Mr. Suro's article have been omitted because of space limitations in the book.]

Dialoging

Addressing facts and opinions are only the first steps toward building a better 2010 for our children. Discussing the information—and personal reflections—with others broadened our thinking, added new ideas, and sometimes challenged cherished personal assumptions. We encourage readers to undertake a similar process: Form a group, discuss this book and your own information with others, and embark on your own journey toward 2010. This section concludes with an overview of the dialogue process and a suggested list of questions for discussion.

The dialogue process

The **Children of 2010** sessions used dialogue as a method of group exploration and discovery. We adopted this approach because it supported an underlying principle—working toward a shared vision within a democracy. We believe that this principle should be central to subsequent dialogues.

William Isaacs writes that "During the dialogue process, people learn to think together—not just in the sense of analyzing a shared problem or creating new pieces of shared knowledge, but in the sense of occupying a collective sensibility, in which the thoughts, emotions, and resulting actions belong not to one individual but to all of them together."[8] Physicist David Bohm has suggested that while fragmentation is a condition of our times, it is dialogue which presents us with an opportunity to step back to reveal connections and common ground.[9] And

Benjamin Barber proposes that through dialogue "We can invent alternative futures, create mutual purposes and construct competing visions of community. (Such) talk is not talk about the world; it is talk that makes and remakes the world."[10]

So, we invite you to engage in dialogue with other people—including individuals who are different in terms of culture, occupation, and opinion.

Questions for further dialogue

1. Which facts surprised you in "Demographic eye-openers?"

2. What can parents do to build a better future for their children?

3. In a society that is becoming more racially and culturally diverse, what do you think our nation should do to be *One America?*

4. Can you offer an incident or news story from the recent past that gives you hope—that all of us in the United States can work and live together as a democracy?

5. What are the implications of immigration for democracy in 2010?

6. What can be done for children and youth who are at risk of experiencing a "Johnny Thomas" life?

7. What social and economic changes do you want to make happen in your lifetime?

8. Can some of the ideas of *dialogue* be applied to democracy?

9. Have you read any other books recently that have good ideas or useful facts for this discussion?

The Knowledge Base: Demographics

Focusing

Scope of the first
dialogue session

At the first dialogue on April 7 to 9, participants explored facts about the children of 2010. Demographers project increasing racial, ethnic, cultural, and language diversity. The majority of the nation's youth in some states will be ethnic minorities. A larger proportion will be from families who speak languages other than English. To build a society where all children can participate in 21st century America, adults and institutions must learn how to respect and affirm individuals who are different. This will require change.

Individual and institutional behavior that accommodates individual differences is crucial to all aspects of a democracy. Understanding these differences is an important first step toward behavior and assumptions that enable all of our children to participate fully in the civic, economic, and educational dimensions of the 21st century.

"There is hope" was an emphasis of the first dialogue. The participants acknowledged the profound problems of racism and injustice still prevalent in our society, but they also noted that dramatic progress has occurred in such areas as desegregation and laws for equal employment opportunity.

The first dialogue session is presented in two parts: This chapter surveys the demographic changes that are forecast, and the next chapter explores the implications of diversity, the prospects for positive change, and access to opportunity.

Multiple layers of
identity

Navajo women and children traditionally wear multiple layers of skirts, according to one participant. The layers represent the self, family, clan, community, tribe, and nation. So, too, the children of 2010 will have multiple identities and needs, and any strategy for change must consider these many layers of characteristics and opportunities.

As a group, participants in the first session grappled with the multiple layers of diversity and commonality among the children of 2010. This ranged from the uniqueness of each child to the challenges that all will face in a global economy. Some discussions focused on the individual and family, while others targeted institutions and "the system." Unresolved issues of social justice and the aspirations of racial and ethnic groups were among the layers identified. There was also an acknowledgment that cultural diversity is an asset that we as a nation have not fully appreciated or applied to community problem solving.

The challenge of opening access to opportunity

A lack of respect for individual differences and cultures has been, and is, an underlying barrier to opportunity for children in our society, and this problem permeated many of the discussions. As an example, one of the participants said that public schools often track large numbers of children of color into nonacademic programs, thereby perpetuating underrepresentation in college admissions and graduation.[11] There is a tendency of our institutions to view difference as a deficit, rather than an asset. One participant noted that this mindset is not universal, referencing a philosophy of development formulated in Italy that views a child's individuality as rich, strong, powerful, and limitless. In such a positive context, differences may be viewed as assets rather than deficits.

The power of inclusiveness

The participants brought many perspectives to the **Children of 2010** session, reflecting a broad range of careers, racial and ethnic groups, and academic backgrounds. The insights of each perspective enabled the group as a whole to see the issues more clearly. Each culture brings values to the table, as well as knowledge, and these were shared as part of the dialogue. Many Native Americans, for example, view the land as sacred and place a high priority on protecting natural resources for the children of the future. Some Hispanics view Spanish as more than a language; it is a means of fostering culture and identity. At the same time, the group also noted that there is diversity within diversity: A great range of perspectives exists within all racial or ethnic groups, and stereotypes are inappropriate and dangerous.

Some of the most striking comments about diversity were from a participant who immigrated to the United States during the 1970s. "I came from a culture where individuals like myself were in the majority. On arriving here, I became a minority. Personal habits that were as ordinary as breathing were brought into question. I found myself explaining things like why I ate rice almost every day."

She said that other nations with ethnic minorities—such as Australia and Canada—organize institutional approaches to address the needs of minority groups. Rather than formal and structured approaches, the United States tends to take an informal, unstructured approach. "The result is often the victim game," where the only recourse is to claim victimization. The victim game is not a positive, self-affirming experience. Further, redress of grievances is often abandoned to the U.S. court system, which results in the polarizing of various groups rather than promoting reconciliation. We need a better way of solving our problems.

Sensitivity to the needs of all children

Caring for the children of 2010 will involve as much sensitivity toward the needs of all children as it will sensitivity toward issues of diversity. Some adults have an "attitude problem" toward children.

Our participants, most of whom work to benefit the lives of young people and foster diversity, see children differently than others in the population might.[12] Since 40% of the adult population does not have a child under 18 living in their household, the consensus of participants was that Americans should be more involved with children.

One problem is that some adults don't like children. We live in a society in which children and youth have a lot of problems, and people become turned off by these problems. They assume they can't do anything to ease these problems and begin to distance themselves from them. "The problem with children," said one participant, "is adults."

Those who distance themselves from children's problems might blame the parents. Instead, the dialogue participants seemed to suggest that those who distance themselves are the problem. Adults who are *involved* with children—parents, teachers, others—are the solution.

But even our participants, who are frequently involved with children, recognize it's not that easy. While some see children as limitless, we sometimes see them in our adult image, and may expect more of them than they are capable of. One participant suggested that the American educational system still doesn't cater enough to children's individual needs.

The children of 2010 will need more affirmation by adults of the value and importance of childhood, and they will need heightened sensitivity and respect for their individuality.

Us vs. them

When children are born, they do not perceive different races. A White participant has a 5-year-old son who chose a Black doll over a White one. The boy lives in a racially mixed environment and perceives some people as simply "darker" than others.

This is an idealistic view. But for this child, certain characteristics of American society will fly in the face of his view.

First, he will meet people with cultural differences and may have to alter some of what he has learned. Throughout the conference, the participants mentioned some of those differences. For example, in White, Anglo-Saxon American society, looking someone in the eye connotes respect. In Asian and Hispanic cultures, this shows disrespect. Hispanic parents might tell their children *never* to look their teacher in the eye; they should look at the ground when she talks to them. These cultures may all have the same notion of respect but observe it in different ways.

Second, this child will meet people who are intolerant. As a member of a minority group, this child will detect when he is seen as inferior. Suddenly, he is caught between what he is taught at home—"you're just as good as everybody else"—and what he experiences in the real world.

A meeting leader expressed this dilemma. As tolerant adults, we prefer to see race as a meaningless social construct largely devoid of "objective meaning." But how do we teach equality to Black children, when they can see that they are treated differently than Whites?

Later in their school careers, however, racial distinctions may become greater. The 5-year-old who sees people as "darker" rather than of a certain race attends a school that is 75% Black. Yet the students in the school's talented and gifted program are 75% White.

Virtually 100% of today's adults believe that members of minority groups should have the same opportunities as members of the majority; in 1943, less than 50% believed this. But the participants cited a less positive study where American workers said they would prefer to work with people who are "like themselves." Another study revealed that people who were alike got along better than people who were not alike.

What is "alike?" Can people be "alike" but be of different races? One participant suggested the dangers of telling children that people of a different race are "just like us." Some people may *choose* to be different, to be themselves. For some people in the United States, tolerance of different groups may be contingent upon "them" being like us.

So, the participant asked, how do we educate (White) children who will give up their majority in the 21st century? How do we explain to them that the new majority (minority children) won't be just like us?

Exploring demographics

The characteristics of the United States population have been in a state of flux for decades and even centuries. In 1908, a Brooklyn teacher wrote

> Dearest Mother,
> Although I enjoy my teaching very much, it is very hectic. There are 28 students in my third grade class. Six speak English; the rest speak a bewildering variety of eight other languages, of which I know a few words of only 3. With the others, we use sign language and get along as best we can. I am working to get parents to translate, but most of them know no English. I hope next year to get a better start with language. . . .[13]

The languages in that Brooklyn classroom were all European. Teachers today may work in classrooms with students who speak Spanish, Asian, African, and other languages. And, during the 20th century, there have been large-scale population movements within the United States: from rural to city, from city to suburb, and from region to region. Diversity today extends far beyond a matter of language.

Diversity is certain, but national unity is a challenge

"*E pluribus* is easy; it's the *unum* that's the challenge." So began a discussion about the demographics of 2010, which is marked by the increasing racial and ethnic diversity of children. The challenge will be for these children—and adults—to find common ground, to craft the next generation's interpretation of "America." The presenter was Dr. Bud Hodgkinson, who directs the Center for Demographic Policy in Washington, D.C.

Global perspective

Population shifts in the United States are occurring within the context of dramatic worldwide changes. Global trends include major population shifts both within and between nations, and migration/immigration is expected to continue as it always has throughout history. Much of the population movement is economically motivated: individuals and families seeking a better standard of living by moving from agrarian areas to cities and other industrial areas, or by immigrating to countries with better-paying jobs and other opportunities for advancement. In some cases, such as immigration to Europe, foreign nationals are compensating for labor shortages caused by the low birth rates prevalent within the countries. According to

Hodgkinson, another trend, worldwide, is that most girls will grow up in societies where they will be engaged in both childrearing and earning a living.

Population outlook for 2010

Hodgkinson said that the number of children under age 18 years in the United States will increase by over 2% between the years 2000 and 2010—from 70.8 million to 72.5 million. During the same period, the young adults in the United States who are between 18 and 44 will decline by over 1%. Mature and older Americans will be the largest gainers in numbers: Those between 45 and 64 will increase by 29%, and the number of individuals who are 65 or older will increase by nearly 14%.

The increase in the number of older Americans is staggering: There will be 17 million **more** adults between 45 and 64, and over 4 million **more** who are 65 or older. These two age groups represent an increase of about 21 million people—compared to an increase of less than 2 million for the population under 18. Thus the additional people aged 45 or older will be roughly comparable to the 1990 population of New York State and Connecticut, while the additional youth will be comparable to the 1990 population of Utah. Figure 2 depicts these trends by age group.

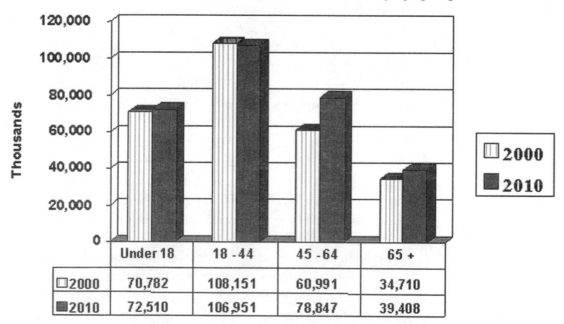

	Under 18	18 - 44	45 - 64	65 +
□2000	70,782	108,151	60,991	34,710
■2010	72,510	106,951	78,847	39,408

Figure 2. U.S. Population Trends by Age, 2000 and 2010
Statistical Abstract of the United States, 1997

Hodgkinson noted that the number of older Americans will increase, and the ages of 50 to 75 will be viewed as only the third quarter of life. Today, there are already 56,000 individuals who are age 100 or older. Life beyond 75 will become an expectation for many.

Long-range projections of population characteristics are not precise, however, and are subject to intervening factors including the economy, changes in life styles and birth rates, immigration policy, and health. An April 1996 article in *American Demographics* magazine, for example, points out that how America ages could vary: "Conventional wisdom says that the share of the U.S. population aged 65 and older should increase into the next century. This is true for the population as a whole, but the extent to which it will happen varies by race and ethnicity."[14]

In general, there will be population growth among all racial and ethnic groups, though the rate of growth will be quite different, and the age distributions within each group will vary. To illustrate, the White population will be considerably older than the Hispanic population. Figure 3 estimates by how many people (in thousands) each group will increase between 2000 and 2010.

Population Increase in Thousands

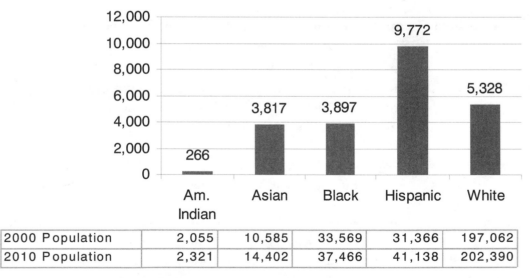

	Am. Indian	Asian	Black	Hispanic	White
2000 Population	2,055	10,585	33,569	31,366	197,062
2010 Population	2,321	14,402	37,466	41,138	202,390

Figure 3. Projected U.S. population increases by race/ethnic group, between 2000 and 2010
White Hispanics are counted as Hispanic.

The rate of population growth varies markedly by racial/ethnic group, and this is the driving force behind projections of increased racial/ethnic diversity among children and youth. Figure 4 depicts the percentage growth of various groups between 2000 and 2010. The percentages are calculated by dividing the estimated increases (Figure 3) for each group by the total population within that group (see data table with Figure 3).

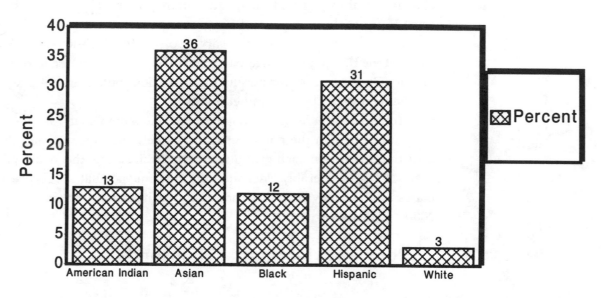

Figure 4. Estimated population growth by race/ethnic group, by percent 2000–2010
White Hispanics are counted as Hispanic.

Recent trends for school-age children

Recent changes in the racial and ethnic composition of school-age populations have been noted in a report by the General Accounting Office (GAO).[15] According to the GAO, the number of non-Hispanic Whites in this population decreased by 4 million (12%) between 1980 and 1990. The Black school population declined by 250,000 (4%), while Hispanics increased by 1.25 million (57%). Asians in the school population rose by 600,000 (87%).

Kids count

Between 1995 and 2005, there will be a five percent increase in the population under 18 years of age. According to data from *Kids Count*[16] (Casey Foundation), cited by Hodgkinson, however, this will not be distributed evenly.

Table 2
Youth Population by Age, 1995–2005

Millions

Age range	1995	2005	NET
0–5	23.6	22.9	-3%
6–11	22.7	23.6	+4%
12–14	11.3	12.6	+12%
15–17	11.0	12.6	+15%
All	*67.7*	*71.9*	*+5%*

Table 3
Youth Population by Race/Ethnic Group, 1995–2005

Millions

Group	1995	2005	NET
American Indian	0.673	0.713	+6%
Asian/PI	2.5	3.5	+39%
Black	10.1	11.0	+8%
Hispanic	9.5	12.4	+30%
Subtotal, people of color	*22.8*	*27.6*	*21%*
White, non-Hispanic	45.7	44.2	-3%
All	*67.7*	*71.9*	*+5%*

Race as a social construct

There is no scientific basis for distinctions between races, Hodgkinson said, and the categories used by the Census Bureau reflect the changes in U.S. social distinctions. As recently as 1960, the Census categories were for Whites and Nonwhites. In 1970, the Nonwhite category was divided into Black and Other. The 1980 Census added three categories: (1) American Indian, Eskimo, Aleut; (2) Asian, Pacific Islander; and (3) Hispanic. The 1990 Census added subcategories for Hispanic and for Asian, Pacific Islander.

While race is a nonscientific set of distinctions, the **Children of 2010** group noted that minority participants at the dialogue session would encounter the "social construct" directly and personally within moments of leaving the meeting room. Hodgkinson noted that one quarter of the "White" population is darker than the lightest quarter of the "Black" population.

"You don't get counted if you aren't born"

Hodgkinson said that the causes for changes in the population count are simple: births, deaths, and immigration. He presented 1995 to 1996 statistics to make the point:

Table 4
U.S. population changes, 1995–1996

Births	3,879,800
Deaths	2,330,900
Immigration	855,600

Hodgkinson pointed out that 43 million Americans move each year. Regarding population migration, the Northeast's population has been declining while the South's has been increasing. Even within regions, there are great variations: Within the West, California has lost population, but the Mountain states have experienced growth. And, a sharp drop in the population in New York State accounts for nearly two-thirds of the decline in the Northeast.

Different birth rates among racial and ethnic groups are a major factor in the changing demographics for the children of 2010. The birth rate for White women is 1.8, while it is 2.6 for Blacks and 3.0 for Hispanics. There are variations within these broad categories, however, such as the high birth rate for White women in Utah. Subgroups within the Hispanic and Asian/Pacific Islander categories have birth rates that may be quite different from the "average."

The changing characteristics of "household"

The nature of the "household" is changing. Only one in four consists of a married couple with one or more school-age children living at home. Another one in four households are individuals living alone. One in eight are single mothers with children. An increasing number of households consists of unrelated individuals. Most households with children are "busy places," because 70% of school-age children have working mothers. Many households do not have daily or weekly contact with children, and in some cases this may affect voter attitudes toward public policy issues affecting children.

Children and poverty

Children under 6 years are more likely to be poor than any other age group of Americans. Of all U.S. children, over 20% are being raised below the poverty line, the highest percentage of any NATO nation. Children are an increasing proportion of America's poor: While only 10% of America's poor were children in 1950, some 40% of the poor were children in 1990. This contrasts sharply with the elderly who, through Social Security or other means, have declined as a proportion of America's poor from 40 to 10% during the same period.

Five out of eight young children who are poor live in households where at least one parent or relative works. Fewer than three out of ten live with parents who are on welfare. Between 1970 and the early 1990s, young-child poverty increased faster in the suburbs than in the central cities.

Ten million Americans—four million of them children—do not have enough to eat. Most are members of families with at least one worker. These families usually lack health insurance, and the head of household usually does not have a high school diploma. One out of six Mexican Americans and one out of 12 Blacks experience hunger. Facts presented here about hunger are from the National Health and Nutrition Examination Survey.[17]

Lessons from anthropology

Diversity encompasses many cultural dimensions that extend far beyond Census Bureau data. One participant illustrated the complexity of relationships by recounting the story of a first grader.

On the first day of school, the boy's mother groomed her son with great care and firmly told him that he must do three things: stand tall, show respect to his teacher, and speak only in English. At school, the Anglo teacher greeted her new students and told them to introduce themselves. She told them that they must follow three rules when giving their introductions: They must stand tall, look straight into her eyes, and give their full name.

When it was the boy's turn, he stammered. He stood tall, like his mother and teacher had told him to do. But to look into his teacher's eyes would show disrespect, and his mother taught him to be respectful. His Mexican name had no English equivalent, and he would have to speak it in Spanish. Within minutes after beginning his first day of school, the boy had violated two of his mother's instructions. He was very sad, because he would return home and confess to his mother that he had failed to meet her expectations.

From an anthropological perspective, Hodgkinson said, diversity is expressed in cultural dimensions, including those identified at the meeting:

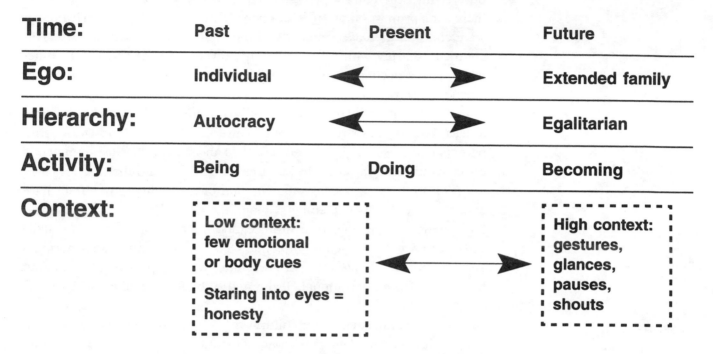

Figure 5. Cultural dimensions
From E. Hall, *The Silent Language*[18]

There are other socio-cultural dimensions that the group explored. One was religion, and the group noted that there are now more Muslims in the United States than Episcopalians. A U.S. map of religious affiliations demonstrated that there was a demographic basis for the term "Bible Belt."[19] Also, the fertility rate for Mormon women is the highest of any "White" group in the world.

Paradigms of race relations

Paradigms seeking to depict race relations through diagrams were introduced for discussion purposes. Several of these are presented in Figure 6. A "Past Paradigm," presented by Hodgkinson, captures the historic White-Black interaction and tension, with sporadic attention to American Indians. Other people of color were usually ignored and left totally outside the box. Hodgkinson recounted a dinner conversation among researchers from diverse backgrounds. During the dinner, several people noted how this paradigm from the past reasserts itself, as it did during the O.J. Simpson trial.

The court drama was like a ping pong game between Whites and Blacks. Everyone else was only a spectator, watching the game from the bleachers. Public opinion, the media, and the reactions of Whites and Blacks were a reenactment of White-Black race relations in America.

The "Current Diversity Paradigm" depicts a collaborative roundtable that is inclusive of all racial and ethnic groups. In all too many cases, the group noted, this inclusive paradigm is more of an ideal than a reality in many communities, workplaces, and programs.

As a group, we are being challenged to take a hard look at our assumptions and the paradigms we apply to problem-solving strategies. In Figure 6, we have therefore left the paradigm for the future open ended, with the intent of revisiting these issues during our second and third sessions.

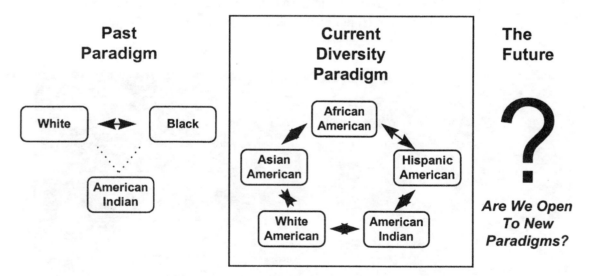

Figure 6. Paradigms of race relations

Race and ethnic relations may be improving

Despite past and present problems in the United States, there are encouraging signs that some progress is being achieved in race relations. Positive indicators during our lifetime include access to schools and public accommodations, the end of segregation in the armed forces, voting rights, the election of many more minority candidates to public office, and broad changes in employer personnel policies.

While *affirmative action* remains controversial among some Whites and some minorities,[20] Hodgkinson said there is almost universal acceptance of the goal of *equal employment opportunity*. For many years, the Gallup Annual Survey has polled Americans on the question "Blacks should have the same chances as Whites to get any kind of job." In 1944, only 45% of poll respondents agreed, but agreement reached 97% by 1995. Gallup surveys also indicate that, today, a majority of Whites and Blacks tell pollsters that they have a close personal friend of the other race.[21]

A bottom-line indicator is that most Americans, regardless of race or ethnic group, believe that the United States is the best place to live. For example, Hodgkinson said that 82% of Whites and 74% of Blacks shared this belief.[22]

Reactions to the presentation on demographics

The presentation about demographics sparked a lively discussion among participants. Some of the points made were

- While people of color—including children and youth—will be gaining numbers through growing populations, change that leads to more opportunities and a better standard of living also requires power and resources.
- Child care workers and teachers need to listen to how each child and family defines identity, for we cannot make assumptions about other people's identities.
- Identity is partly a matter of how other people respond to us.
- How many young people of color have friends who belong to other minority groups?
- Several of the broadly defined racial and ethnic groups contain a great deal of diversity. In terms of demographics, for example, there are significant differences between Mexican Americans, Puerto Ricans, Cubans, and other Latinos. Yet, there is a language and customs that generally bind these subgroups together. Moreover, a need to come together as a means for exercising political power may be the most important rationale for identity with the overall Hispanic group.
- How do we explore the issue of coming together as an inclusive society when there is yet so much healing and achievement to be done within each group?
- It isn't possible to implement inclusiveness until we address the issues of racism.
- Individuals with handicaps and disabilities must be part of the picture for inclusiveness.
- Americans will have a distorted picture of their community and country for as long as newspapers and broadcasters fail to achieve inclusiveness as a personnel policy.
- The histories and values of our various races and cultures do not need to negate each other. There can be respect and honor for all.
- One in four marriages today is outside of the same cultural/racial group.
- How do you educate White children to give up their privileges when you *do not* say other people are just like them—or are trying to become just like them? Suppose you reject an assimilationist melting-pot model and, instead, opt for a model that affirms diversity. Can you sell White kids on the idea that they are just a piece of the American puzzle rather than the whole picture?

- How fearful or defensive will Whites become in communities or states where people of color outnumber them at the polls, on the job, or in the schools?
- It is so very easy to be blind about the needs of other people. It is like building a house with front steps—a "normal" and everyday practice, until you discover a disabled friend struggling to gain entrance. As individuals and institutions, we frequently build thoughtless and unnecessary "steps" that are barriers to children and youth.
- How do we keep the focus on children rather than [inter-group] politics?

The flip side of the demographics coin

A number of social commentators have painted gloomy pictures of the future because of the changing demographics, evident among the children of 2010 but extending through projections to 2050 as well. A challenge to both the dialogue participants and Americans everywhere is to respond with a balanced approach which (1) takes the potential problems seriously and initiates appropriate corrective actions but (2) avoids a self-fulfilling prophecy of doom and gloom.

We know that self confidence, aspirations, and a positive self image are important to the healthy development of children. However, gloomy scenarios can spawn hopelessness, fear, and low expectations, both for individual children and our society as a whole. Therefore, the dialogue group said it was important to identify the opportunities, as well as the problems, among the demographic data. The following list was offered as thought-starters:

Diversity is already working in some communities, schools, and workplaces. While isolated and sometimes imperfect, real-world solutions are emerging.

People of color will have increasing influence as voters and customers. Increasingly, survival in elected office or the marketplace will require greater attention to the preferences and customs of many diverse groups.

There will be increasing diversity in elective office, many professions and technology careers, and senior management positions—even though the immediate increases may fall far short of parity.

The United States is positioned to benefit greatly from a *global economy* because it is one of the few nations on earth that has a labor force reflecting the people, cultures, races, and languages of the world. To do business in the world of tomorrow will require Americans who can relate to and communicate with individuals from many other nations.

Higher birth rates among a number of minority groups and immigration to the United States have helped American industry avoid labor shortages—a crisis in a number of European countries that have resorted to importing labor (through special work permits).

Older White Boomers must rely increasingly on people of color to provide their health care. Quality care (and longevity) for older people will require thorough preparation of future health workers, including good schools and children's services.

U.S. technology companies will face a crisis if they cannot recruit enough skilled workers who have appropriate preparation in science, mathematics, and interpersonal communication. They need child development programs, communities, and schools that prepare the children of 2010 for these jobs.

A new generation of employers are establishing a *meritocracy,* where competent individuals who perform are rewarded handsomely, regardless of formal academic credentials. This is an extra avenue of opportunity, including for individuals who have not done well in traditional schooling, provided community resources foster high-tech competencies among young people.

Who will buy the homes of retiring White Boomers unless increased numbers of minority group members have the income levels necessary to make the purchases? The real estate market, which represents much of the life savings of many Boomers, could be a disaster without the economic empowerment of people of color.

Diversity opens opportunities for White children, some of whom have not done well in the rigid, traditional process of public education. White children, as well as others, need more recognition of and response to their individual differences.

Many Whites want to "do the right thing" even if they are confused or awkward in implementing their commitment.

Some American businesses are already finding that it is profitable to embrace diversity. A case in point is Snyder Communications, founded 10 years ago by a White 23-year-old college dropout who in 1996 was the youngest person to head a company listed on the New York Stock Exchange. Daniel Snyder, CEO, has lead his marketing company of 8,000 employees to niche populations such as young adults, racial and ethnic minorities, and international people. According to an article in *The Washington Post:*[23]

Customers say this targeted approach is working. GTE Communications Corp. recently signed a three-year contract with Snyder worth $200 million, for help in selling its long-distance services to ethnic customers. This direct marketing is mostly done through face-to-face meetings rather than those telemarketing calls than often interrupt a potential customer's dinner.

"Results have exceeded expectations so far," said Ed Miller, GTE's director for ethnic and international marketing. "We are just thrilled." He said Snyder is well positioned to reach this target population, noting that its employees speak more than a dozen languages.

Snyder said his company owes its growth to a number of trends in the marketplace and to a willingness to listen to its clients. Among the trends that have benefited his business: . . . the increasing ethnic and racial diversity of the population, which makes advertising more difficult.

Reflecting

She Is America
by Jim Kendrick

She is America.
Visions in her infant eyes dance
like fireflies laughing at the dark:
>   red dreams
>   brown dreams
>   black dreams
>   white dreams
>   yellow dreams,

all dreams of freedom in a youthful land,
where hope defies the thunder
to reach for stars beyond.

She is America.
In her childish whisper
the mother tongue of a hundred nations:
>   Ojibwe
>   Spanish
>   Zulu
>   Greek and
>   Mandarin;

five thousand years and more to speak
of knowledge gained and kingdoms built,
of joy and blood, tears and song.

She is America.
Offspring of ten thousand dreams,
mind restless, relentless to question
our past, her future:
>   millennial vision
>   nanosecond silicon
>   open democracy
>   global neighborhood
>   and sisterhood.

Brash nation where fresh ink of history
has yet to dry, and change
is called American ingenuity.

She is America,
and we are her parents, her past,
a dowry for tomorrow.
>   The sky and prairie
>   song and family
>   soul and freedom
>   hope and laughter
>   roots and future.

Come sing with her so she can dance
to the salsa beat of nations
in nations in democracy.

For she is America.

Broadening the
definition of diversity

The concept of diversity is broadening. The text below is from the book *Winning with Diversity* by Donald M. Norris and M. C. Joelle Fignole Lofton.[24] Figure 7 is an adaptation of a diagram in the book.

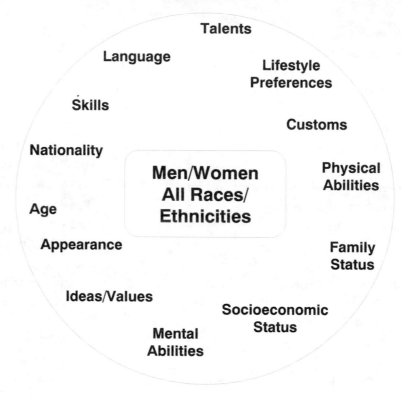

Figure 7. The marketplace model: cultural diversity

Diversity means difference. In its earliest definition, valuing diversity meant understanding and valuing the characteristics and capabilities of a narrowly defined set of targeted racial, ethnic, and gender groups—blacks, Hispanics, Native Americans,/Pacific Islanders, and women. Diversity simply meant people in these groups.

Over time, however, the definition of diversity expanded to include a wider range of ethnic and racial characteristics, including age, physical abilities, family status, lifestyle preferences, socioeconomic status, religious and spiritual values, language, and geographic location. Organizations have tried to create work environments that are friendly to the full range of people displaying these characteristics. White males have been included among the groups requiring consideration as components of diversity and treated as part of the solution, not as the problem.

In addition to adding new characteristics to the concept of diversity, we've come to understand that any particular group will exhibit a tremendous range of values and characteristics. One size does not fit all: Group stereotypes have no place in the 1990s organization.

Under this more sophisticated definition, diversity includes every employee, member, and customer. Each must be afforded the respect of being treated as someone whose wants and needs will be understood and addressed. Everyone in the organization must develop the awareness necessary to achieve this level of understanding. In today's diverse organization, every person has a great deal to learn. . . .

Reprinted from *Winning with Diversity* with permission from ASAE.

The Math Behind Race

by John Allen Paulos[25]

Who can forget the morass of statistics used in the O.J. Simpson double-murder trial? What did the cited DNA probabilities mean? Did the jury and the public grasp the mathematics undergirding the numbers?

More recently, the issues of race, death and mathematics have again subtly intertwined. This time, the misunderstanding arises because the technical meaning of a common phrase differs substantially from its informal meaning. What at first glance may seem like semantic nitpicking has significant consequences for public policy and perceptions.

In a study published in *The Times*, there appeared a potentially inflammatory, although ostensibly correct, statement. In reporting on death sentences in Philadelphia, the study asserted that the odds of blacks convicted of murder receiving a death sentence were four times the odds faced by other defendants similarly convicted. The *Times* article, as well as accounts in other newspapers, then transmuted that statement into the starkly inequivalent one that blacks were four times as likely to be sentenced to death as whites. The author of the study used the technical definition of odds, not the more familiar idea of probability, and, as a consequence, most readers were seriously mislead.

The difference between "probability" and "odds" is crucial. The odds of an event is defined as the probability it will occur divided by the probability that it will not occur. Consider a coin flip. The probability of its landing heads is one-half, or .5, and the probability of not landing heads is also one-half, or .5.

Hence: The odds of the coin landing heads is 1 to 1 (.5 divided by .5). Now consider rolling a die and having it land on 1,2,3,4 or 5. The probability of this event is five-sixths, or .83, and the probability of the die not landing on 1,2,3,4 or 5 is one-sixth, or .17. Hence: The odds of the die landing on one of these five numbers is 5 to 1 (.83 divided by .17). More serious discrepancies between probabilities and odds occur for events with higher probabilities.

What's the relevance of this to murder statistics and death penalties? To most readers, the phrase "four times the odds" means that if, say, 99% of blacks convicted of murder were to receive the death penalty, about 25% of whites similarly convicted would receive the same penalty.

Yet, when the technical definition of "odds" is used, the meaning is quite different. In this case, if 99% of blacks convicted of murder received the death penalty, then a considerably less unfair 96% of whites similarly convicted would receive the death penalty. Why? Using the technical definition, we find that the odds in favor of a convicted black murderer getting death are 24 to 1 (96/100 divided by 4/100). Thus, since 99 is roughly four times 24, the odds that a convicted black murderer will receive the death penalty are, in this case, approximately four times the odds that a convicted nonblack murderer will receive the same sentence.

According to the study, in 667 Philadelphia murder cases from 1983 to 1993 that could have produced death sentences, 520 defendants were black and 147 were white. Ninety-five of the black defendants—roughly 18 per-cent—and 19 of the whites—roughly 13 percent—were sentenced to death. In other words, black defendants were about 40 percent (not four times, as the L.A. Times put it) more likely than whites to get the death penalty.

As Arnold Barnett and others have shown, similarly misleading claims were made in the 1987 U.S. Supreme Court decision in McClesky vs. Kemp. The issue concerned the effect of a murder victim's race on death sentenc-ing in the state of Georgia, but the confusion is the same.

By dissecting the phrase "four times the odds," I don't mean to deny that racism exists, that there are racial disparities in sentencing or that the death penalty is morally wrong. Rather, I mean to deflate the likely-to-be-inferred magnitude of racial disparities in the sentencing for murder and other violent crimes. The difference between 99% and 96%, for example, is much less egregious than that between 99% and 25%. Still, whatever they are, the raw percentages are troubling enough without the tendentious and easily misinterpreted phrase "four times the odds."

Reprinted with permission of the author. As published in the *Los Angeles Times* on July 12, 1998, but with the addition of a paragraph on raw data, as requested by Mr. Paulos.

Children in poverty by state

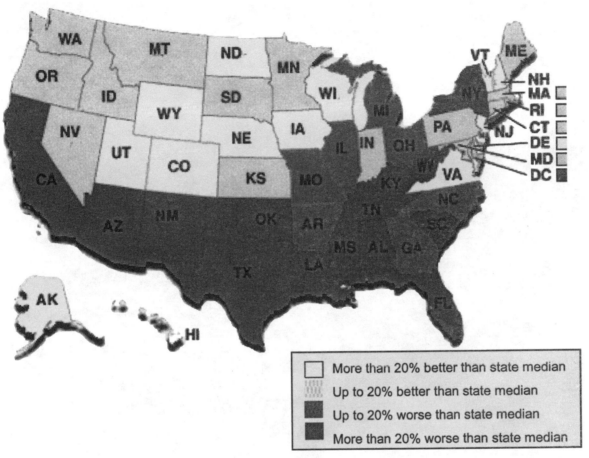

Figure 8. Percent children in poverty by state
From *Kids Count,* 1997; Annie B. Casey Foundation

Projected Anglo
population

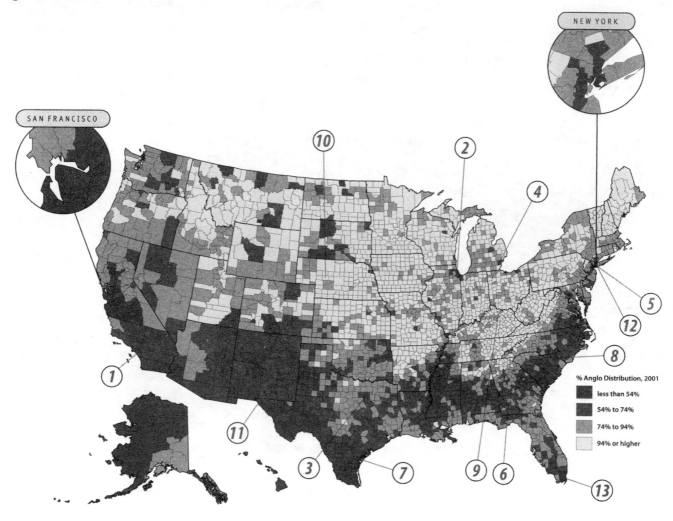

Figure 9. Projected Anglo population for U.S. counties in 2001

Reprinted from *Diversity in America* with permission. © 1997, PRIMEDIA/Intertec, Stamford, CT.

Projected Asian population

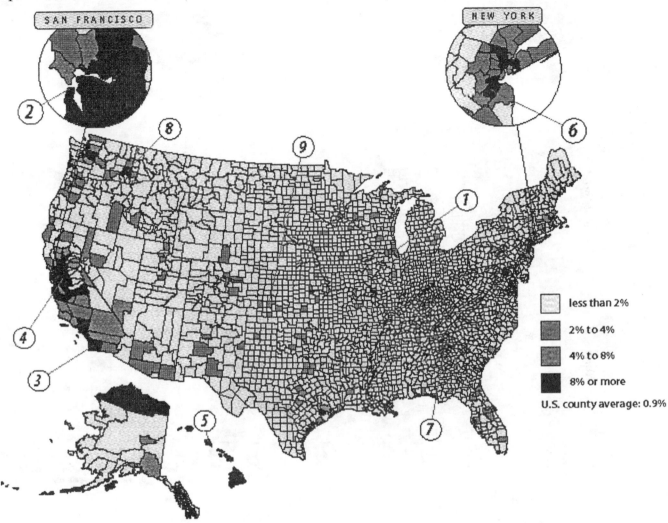

Figure 10. Projected Asian population for U.S. counties in 2001

Reprinted from *Diversity in America* with permission. © 1997, PRIMEDIA/Intertec, Stamford, CT.

Projected Black
population

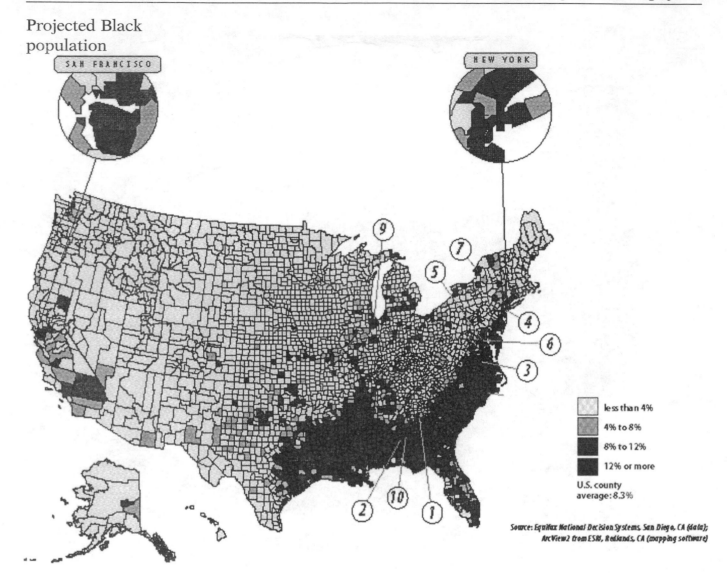

Figure 11. Projected Black population for U.S. counties in 2001
Reprinted from *Diversity in America* with permission. © 1997, PRIMEDIA/Intertec, Stamford, CT.

Projected Hispanic map

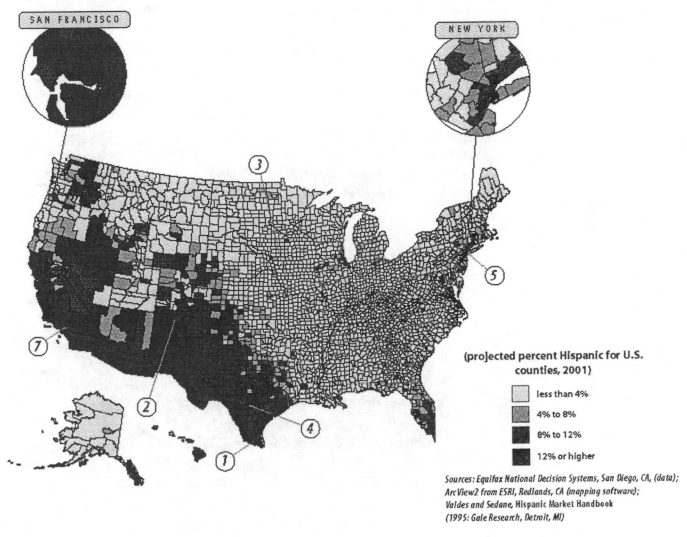

Figure 12. Projected Hispanic population for U.S. counties in 2001

Reprinted from *Diversity in America* with permission. © 1997, PRIMEDIA/Intertec, Stamford, CT.

Dialoging about demographics

This chapter has addressed the demographic changes that are underway in the United States. Some of the questions that you may want to explore as part of a group are

1. Looking at the maps, which regions of the country will experience the most dramatic changes in demographics?

2. Updated reports about demographic and economic trends are available on a continued basis. Ask someone in your dialogue group to check for new data at the Census Bureau's web site: http://www.census.gov. In addition to national data, look for new information that may be available about your state or community.

3. What is the outlook for the state where you live?

4. How have demographics changed in your community over the past 20 years? Have they changed in your workplace and the organizations to which you belong?

5. Demographers forecast even more diversity during the 21st century. How do you think programs for children and youth should respond?

6. Within your own racial/ethnic group, can you think of some stereotypes that do not fit? Can you think of ways in which there is a great deal of diversity within your group?

7. What is your reaction to "The Math Behind Race"? Do you think that statistics are sometimes misused in discussions about race and fairness?

8. Figure 6 is a paradigm of race relations. Do you agree with how the "past" and "present" paradigms are depicted? What do you believe the paradigm might be for the future?

9. For a long time, the United States has been viewed as a nation of immigrants. Do you see any differences in the situation of immigrants now, compared to a century ago?

10. Figure 7, the marketplace model, broadens "diversity" to address many dimensions beyond race, culture, and language. What model of diversity do you think will best address the needs of the children of 2010?

The Knowledge Base: Diversity, Change, and Opportunity

Focusing

Change is nothing new. The population of the North American continent in 1410, 1710, and 2010 would produce dramatically different social, economic, linguistic, and demographic profiles. Each era of inhabitants has been confronted by change. What is unique to 2010, however, is our evolving vision of democracy. Transforming the vision of inclusive, participatory change into reality is a challenge for our generation, as well as for future children. In the last chapter, we surveyed demographics and the population changes that are continuing to occur. During the first dialogue session, we also explored the implications of diversity, the prospects for positive change, and access to opportunity for the children of 2010.

Exploring: Hispanics and language

Education

The Latino experience became the lens through which dialogue participants surveyed implications of changing demographics. Access to educational opportunity is a crucial issue, because it has a profound impact on economic empowerment and access to leadership positions in community institutions. In addition to education, the participants surveyed such matters as language and culture.

"At no time in the history of the United States has education paid off so well as it does in 1998," stated Dr. Harry Pachon, President of the Thomas Rivera Policy Institute.[26] He said that preventing just two high-school dropouts would benefit a community by $1.5 million over their lifetime.

Pachon said it is particularly important for minority students to gain a good education because 20% of the workforce is engaged in "knowledge work"—also termed symbolic manipulation—the primary beneficiary of high wages and rising incomes. The 80% of the workforce engaged in service or industrial occupations could face low wages and the possibility of stagnant incomes. Citing the books of former Secretary of Labor Robert Reich, the income gap between these types of occupations has widened since 1979. Minorities could find themselves continuing to be concentrated on the wrong side of the "great economic divide" unless there is greater access to educational preparation and high-opportunity careers.

Educational attainment is strongly associated with lifetime income, as depicted in a chart presented by Pachon (Figure 13). On average, a person with a postgraduate education can expect three times the earnings of a high-school dropout.

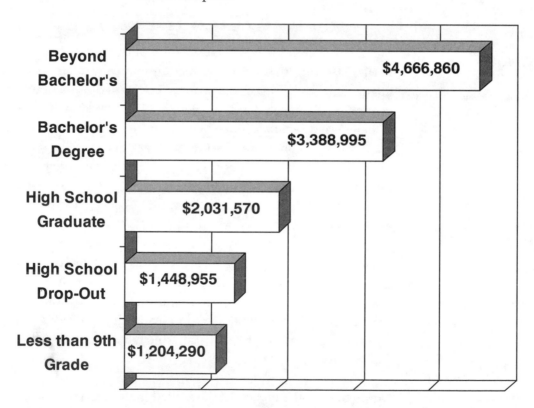

Figure 13. Average lifetime income (45 years) by educational attainment of householder

Another way to view the importance of education is to consider the percentage of the U.S. population in poverty by educational attainment. In Figure 14, *Kids Count* (1997) provides the following figure, based on a special Census count:

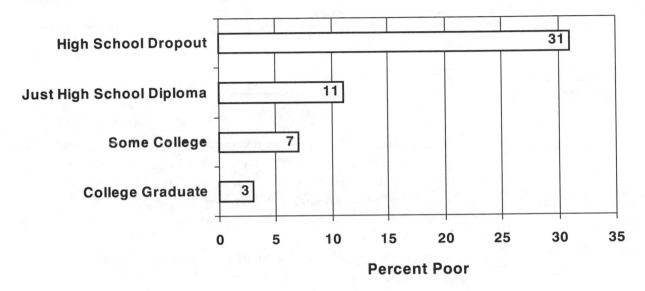

Figure 14. Poverty by educational attainment for persons 25–54 in 1995

The economic challenge
Basically, the challenge is to raise the median wage and help people in the bottom 60% of the workforce do far better than they have done to date.

—Robert B. Reich[27]
Former Secretary of Labor

An alarming problem is the extent to which the public school system places minority students in non-college tracks. In California, for example, Pachon noted, most high school students who are Hispanic or Black do not take algebra, a subject required for admission to the University of California system.

Unless there are dramatic improvements to the educational preparation of children and youth, there will be tragic mismatches between job requirements and the qualifications of the potential labor force. In Los Angeles County alone, there could be over 200,000 fewer college graduates than employers are seeking in the year 2015. Yet, there could be 174,000 more high school dropouts in 2015 than jobs for which they qualify. The details of the projection are in Table 5.

Table 5
Supply-demand mismatch in 2015
Los Angeles County

	High-school dropout	High-school graduate	Some college	College graduate
Supply	1,058,820	928,887	1,856,540	1,195507
Demand	884,106	890,383	1,580,286	1,402,684
Difference	174,714	38,504	276,255	-207,177

Tough questions and comments

The implications of increased diversity sparked a lively discussion. Participants raised probing questions for which there are few quick answers. These ranged from issues regarding families and teacher preparation to broad problems like social justice. A summary follows.

- What are we doing to educate the teachers who will prepare the children of 2010?
- Why aren't public high schools preparing more Hispanics and African Americans for college?
- We discuss "knowledge base," but don't we also need to speak of values? Knowledge alone will not solve the challenges of 2010.
- Will racial and ethnic minorities fight over a small piece of the economic and political pie, or will they work together for a fair share of the pie?
- Why don't minority people in the media work together more frequently?
- Spending on education (adjusted for inflation) may be declining while the minority student population is rising.
- Why have we not discussed the environment and natural resources? Passing the land and the sky and the water along to our children is so very important.
- How do we bring older Whites on board to be part of the solution?
- Should our generation be responsible for resolving injustices in housing, education, and the economy? It would be a terrible thing to pass these devastating problems along to the children of 2010.
- Exactly what is effective in promoting social justice in this country?
- How do you change the dynamic from injustice to opportunity?
- Why is it so difficult to talk about diversity and social justice? It has taken us so much time at this session—simply to find a common language to discuss the issues. We've been making headway, but the process is tedious.

Language: more tough questions and comments

Participants explored issues of language and bilingualism in some detail. Much of the attention focused on the large number of Americans who are Hispanic, but the group also noted that children in the United States come from homes that speak many different languages. Asian Americans/Pacific Islanders, for example, speak a variety of languages. The same is true for Africa, the Middle East, Europe, and many other parts of the world. As a means of summarizing the discussion, we have included some of the questions and comments:

- Kenneth Clark said that schools must be an oasis of acceptance. How can a school practice acceptance if it rejects a child's language?
- Businesses are issuing multilingual manuals. Banks are communicating with customers in multiple languages. Why cannot public institutions do the same?
- In a multilingual world, wouldn't all students benefit from being bi- or tri-lingual?
- In a country that needs more citizens who are fluent in multiple languages, why are the schools discouraging other languages?
- Why don't public agencies and schools make better use of the language skills of parents and others in the community?
- Why would a California school district recruit a bilingual teacher from Spain when there are so many capable bilingual residents within the state?

The danger of myths

Misinformation is a barrier to inclusiveness in a society of diversity, and minority racial and ethnic groups are subject to pervasive myths and misunderstanding. To drive this point home, Pachon focused on myths affecting Latinos. His points are summarized in the following table:

Table 6
Myths about the Latino/Hispanic population

Myth	Fact
Impermanence. Many perceive Hispanics as transient, taking advantage of American benefits only to return to their home country.	In reality, 88% of Hispanics said they preferred the United States to their home country, and 98% of those said they are here to stay.
Homogeneity. The Latino/Hispanic population is homogeneous. (Hispanics are all alike.)	There are major differences between generations, country of origin, education, and income levels. For example, Mexican Americans and Puerto Ricans have demographics that are different from Cuban Americans.
Nonparticipation. Hispanics are nonparticipatory.	Interviews with Hispanics revealed that they were involved in more community groups than non-Hispanic Whites.
Child care programs are unnecessary because Latino mothers and extended families are available for child care.	Like other Americans, Latina mothers often work outside of the home. 28% of Latina mothers report losing a job because there is no child care available. Like other Americans, Latinos prefer family over commercial child care, but that is often not available as an option. Moreover, the Hispanic "extended family" as a resource for child care is not as common in reality as it is in media portrayals.
Latino men do not provide child care.	They do.
Spanish is the preferred language of all Latinos.	Communicating with the Hispanic population requires both Spanish and English: A third is Spanish monolingual, a third is bilingual, and a third is English monolingual. However, 94% of Hispanic parents want their child to speak English, according to one panelist.

Growth of the Hispanic population

There are 20 million Latinos in the United States; by 2020, there will be that many in California alone. "The Latino population," said Pachon, "rather than being *them*, will be *us*, in 2015." It means that Hispanics are now being considered in the diversity equation. In 2010, over one-third of Latinos will be under 18 and over half will be under 25. Children, then, will be an integral part of the positive development of American Hispanics.

As the most populous minority group, in the future, the Hispanic population must be nurtured. The participants acknowledged the concerns—such as the lower educational level of some Hispanic populations—and recognized Hispanics as key players in future diversity. Mexican American and Puerto Rican children are less likely to stay in school than their non-Hispanic White counterparts. And most are also ill prepared for college. Less than 5% of Latino high school students take college prep courses, Pachon said. The recent dismantling of affirmative action in California and Texas—states with large Hispanic populations—was considered one cause, but one participant proposed that the group start searching for other reasons.

Workers in communities with changing demographics

At the community level, changes in race and ethnicity can lead to sensitive issues about the personnel who work for public and nonprofit agencies, because the employees may reflect the previous population. A health clinic in California was cited as an example, where African Americans dominate the management positions but the clientele has become Latino.

On the one hand, the new population needs to participate in community institutions. On the other hand, there needs to be respect for the work and commitment of the incumbent employees. Developing realistic solutions to this type of tension will be an important ingredient for achieving a diverse society where communities and workers accommodate each other by devising and applying win-win strategies.

Job pinch among people of color

With the rapidly increasing population of Hispanics, other minorities might sometimes feel the pinch. As Latinos demand more Latino employees, the displacement of African-Americans in the workforce may follow in some communities. At the time of the conference, *The Washington Post* published an article about Martin Luther King hospital in California, originally run and built primarily by African-Americans. It was built to remedy a troublesome lack of available health care in the Black community. But because Hispanics have become the majority in that neighborhood, there has been an increase in Hispanic patients, many of whom demand Hispanic doctors. Some Blacks object, feeling that the hospital bore the fruits of their own labor rather than the lobbying of Hispanics.

This issue is far from being resolved. The panel conceded that much animosity remains between people of different racial and ethnic backgrounds. However, working together to broaden access to opportunities and options for all Americans may ultimately be a more productive course of action.

Language persists as a national issue

As do Hispanic children, all bilingual children experience more by communicating with different people in different ways. As one participant put it, "There's nothing more fundamental than language. It's how we think, how we perceive ourselves, how we understand society."

Yet according to the participant, the United States is the only developed country in which a monolingual person is considered educated. American schools tend to have low aspirations regarding language skills for students.

One participant referred to a book by Paul Simon, former Democratic senator from Illinois.[28] Simon wrote how monolingualism limits America in many ways. Even large Spanish-speaking regions of the country—Miami, for instance—offer English as a Second Language programs, but not bilingual programs.

Clearly, America has a need for more Spanish speakers. One Hispanic participant said she became a teacher only because people actually went into the *barrios* to offer scholarships to its residents. Some of the 94% who want their children to learn English will need to be reached in Spanish.

A problem arises in cities like Los Angeles, where schools often teach children speaking dozens of different languages. In a country with so many languages, how can so many people possibly be represented? One participant suggested that it's *not* possible to represent all those languages, so America might be better off teaching just English.

The participants reached no consensus on the language issue, but most seemed to support having more social service workers who can reach out to different language communities. Regarding language in the schools, though, one participant acknowledged that most of them probably supported bilingualism. But we might want to approach the issue without the assumption that bilingual education is a good thing, he said.

What the participants might have proven was that the United States is so diverse that the issue of language is a complicated one needing further discussion. Hopefully, such a discussion will lead to a consensus about an approach that benefits the children of 2010.

Positive change and access to opportunity

"What equipment do kids need to advance in our society?" This was both a question and a challenge advanced by one of two youth presenters at the dialogue session.

Unequal competitions

The presenter likened advancement to a track competition or race. Suppose you gave one kid Nike sneakers, another roller blades, and a bicycle to the third kid? The kids can't do equally well in the competition because they have access to different equipment. We aren't giving minority kids and poor kids access to the right equipment. Yet we expect them to compete with kids who have better equipment, and our society is apt to blame them rather than the shoddy equipment if they don't do well in the competition.

She asked Whites in the room if they could accept the fact that they had White privilege. Many Whites are given a sports car for the competition and, sure enough, they are likely to advance quickly to the finish line.

In addition to equipment, she said, every kid needs to know the rules of the game. "You can't advance in our society's systems . . . education, skills, experience, careers . . . unless you know how the system works. Most of the rules are artifacts of White society; kids from other cultures may not have a clue about how these rules work . . . or how the rules will affect them personally."

However, she said that it wasn't just a thing between Whites and people of color. "Can we talk about the Hispanic-Black thing? When we talk about a rule or policy issue, we need to look at how it affects all of the other stakeholders."

The youth presenter scanned the participants and remarked, "In 2010, I want your job." She added, however, that she hoped we would solve some of the problems on the table so that, in the future, she could move on to other items on the agenda.

Respect

The other youth presenter, probed the meaning of *respect*. Recently appointed director of the University of Virginia's summer Bridge program which serves incoming first year minority engineering students, he recounted his past experiences in intervening between instructors and students. Some of the adults just don't get it, he said. They don't take time to listen to students, and they don't see the differences in values that diverse cultures bring.

A case in point was an African American student who had recently dropped a course and was warned that he would have a hard time dropping another one. But in the face of increasing family problems, the student was forced to request another drop. The dean wouldn't hear of it. As an African-American himself, our participant was able to serve as a liaison between the student and the dean—and using the dean's "language" of understanding, he was able to convince him to let the student drop the course.

"I had to explain the importance of the situation to the faculty member, who was forcing the student to make a choice between getting an education and taking care of his parents. The faculty member finally accommodated the student's needs, but all too often schools impose inflexible rules that discourage students of color."

In a land of diversity, he continued, we cannot determine, a priori, how to show respect. We need to ask the students, "What is respect?" For different individuals, respect may need to be expressed in different ways. Every day, all of us need to take the time to appreciate the individuality of each child, each family, each co-worker, for only then can we truly show respect.

The presenter reminded us that respecting children implicitly means respecting their families as well. "Today, this includes diverse races and languages, grandparents, gays, singles, and interracial couples."

Fighting the big flush

The presenter also recalled how public schools had targeted him for a non-academic track while he was in middle school, despite the fact that his abilities and performance were above average. The tracking was simply because he looked different. He was able to enter an academic track in high school only because he and his family were proactive in "beating the system."

In discussions with participants, he wondered how many hundreds, thousands, or millions of children with above-average abilities are flushed down the non-academic drains because of their color, their language, their culture.

Negative stereotyping

The young panelist is a respected liaison between college students and administrators. But as a minority, the world sees him differently when he's not playing that role. "I'm the man in that classroom," he said. "But as soon as I walk out that door, I'm not the man anymore."

He says it took resilience to get to where he is today. By seventh grade, he said, teachers dismissed him as a poor student who would never amount to much. But he fought back.

He warned against "tracking" a schoolchild, which could make them feel less worthy of succeeding on their own. "Don't tell him you can't do something," he said. "Give them support, give them love." He said that not all children are like he was; that is, not all children can fight back.

Pots and bowls

The student presenter said he did not want to be part of an American Melting Pot. He likes his identity, is proud of his heritage, and plans to embrace his uniqueness throughout adulthood. To him, assimilation into a homogeneous society—most likely a mold cast by White Americans—is a distasteful idea. Only the dreaded Borg Collective assimilates races and cultures, and they merely exist in fiction (Star Trek).

"I want America to be a salad bowl," he said. Look at a tossed salad. You can still identify the lettuce, tomato, cucumber, radish, onion, and parsley. Each is unique, and each contributes something to the whole.

She's a child, not a data point

He warned the group about the danger of devising a strategy for the children of 2010 based simplistically on survey results and demographic data. "People love to live off numbers, and that's scary. We treat kids and others based on numbers: tests, grades, surveys, demographics."

Each child has a right to be treated as unique. Each has a right to choices and opportunities. However, institutions tend to use scores and numbers in a way that constricts or eliminates the choices available to many children.

"Before you tell me the data," he said, "tell me who designed the survey or test." The data may be erroneous or inappropriate, even though it is surrounded by the trappings of science. Depending on how you construct the questions and measurement instruments, you can predetermine the resulting answers. Moreover, many researchers will have an agenda that is less than objective.

Many children are victimized by "scientific data." Educators and policymakers must be cautious regarding the ways in which they use data.

The system

Change the system or beat the system?

If the system does not provide children with equal opportunity, one youth participant said, then adults should encourage them to manipulate the system for their own benefit. "If you know the rules of the game, then you can beat the system," he said. For instance, to be accepted, minority children may need to prove themselves more than others do—academically, socially—but in the long run, that extra effort will allow them to grow to their full potential.

Participants at the dialogue had divergent opinions about how to deal with "the system"—the web of institutional practices, policies, and social customs that perpetuate injustice and unequal access to opportunity for children, youth, and their families.

Some saw a system where people of color need a better understanding of the rules and tools for "beating the system." While long-range social change is desirable, they felt that children of today and tomorrow could not wait "for the system to fix itself," for they urgently need help in surviving and advancing now, in an imperfect world.

Others felt that a focus on "beating the system" would lead to "Band Aid" thinking that falls short of solving the underlying problems. One participant discussed an analogy: A large number of people were being pushed into a deep river and drowning. Critics were blaming the victims for failing to have better swimming skills. On a hill across the river, "the system" was a perpetual motion machine, pushing thousands more people into the river. Our dilemma is that, with scarce resources, we are often confronted by the terrible choice of deciding whether to rescue the victims who are drowning now, teach swimming skills, or to change the system so people are not pushed into the river in the future.

"You need to learn the system before you can change it" was one response. Children need life skills about how to survive—in the school system, on the job, in the economy. This requires a strong foundation, and we are failing to share these skills with many of our children.

Another perspective was that "The system belongs to everyone," suggesting that we, collectively and inclusively, take ownership of it.

Empowering children

Children need a lot of positive reinforcement. All too often we are not empowering them.

We must have high expectations for all children, but flexibility in working with children who do not meet them. Because each child is unique and special, we must also construct high expectations that are responsive to each child's individuality.

All children are limitless. Dare we implement such a vision?

The first step to empowering children is to create a community of respect. Ask children: What does respect mean to you? The youth panelist posed this question to the participants, some of whom responded with similar answers:

• Appreciating other people

- Sharing with other people
- Listening to other people / employing "active listening"
- Dignity of self and others
- Acknowledging the values of others
- Treating everyone as individuals
- Fostering equality, but interest in differences
- Making decisions on their own merit, sometimes without the help of others
- High regard for myself and others
- Integrity
- The "Golden Rule": "Do unto others as you would have them do unto you." Though the wording of this varied, this was the most common response.

One participant said that a key factor was missing from these definitions. Most talked about *getting* respect, albeit giving respect as part of that equation. But, this participant asked, doesn't respect need to be earned?

This dilemma was not solved. Some suggested that children need not earn respect; the respect between a teacher and a student should be *a priori*. But, said the mother of the 5-year-old, if we come into contact with children, we're *all* teachers. This discussion indicated that definitions of empowering words—such as "respect"—differ when discussing children rather than adults.

And children who are treated with respect are more likely to give it themselves. "Children didn't ask to be born," reminded one participant, who said that children should be allowed to grow in all areas. One conclusion could be that children need time to earn respect.

Indeed, even points of agreement were interpreted on many levels. When one participant was asked for one thing that everyone could agree upon, one answer was, "Children shouldn't suffer." However, another participant reminded the group that "suffering" could be interpreted in many ways; e.g., is spanking suffering? Here, it seemed evident that concentrating on points of agreement was less important than focusing on everyone's concerns.

"All too often," said one youth participant, "we're not empowering children. We're creating victims." He encouraged empowering children early: he has heard of very young children learning how to write a résumé.

He suggested making children a part of their own learning process. Ask them: What are you interested in? What do you like to do? In what order would you like to do them? These are qualities in the best educational environment, but not all children have equal access to such an environment.

Principles

Participants in the dialogue began to explore the types of principles that could provide an appropriate framework for a **Children of 2010 vision.** Those discussed included

- Children should be free from suffering.
- All children and families deserve respect.
- The individuality and uniqueness of every person should be honored.
- The system belongs to everyone.
- All children should have access to the tools necessary to develop and advance themselves.

Action

"We are accountable—our generation—to get something done before we turn over the mantle to the next generation."

There was broad agreement within the group that—at future sessions—discussion should lead to strategy, and strategy to action. The overriding question, to be answered at the forthcoming sessions, was "Are we bold enough to overcome the way things are . . . and create a different, better future?"

One of the youth representatives expressed the need for action by stating that it was time for all of the participants to put their tools on the table. Each person at the session represented organizations with resources, and these were needed for solving problems and taking action.

"The organizations represented in the room are not carbon copies of each other, and agendas and priorities will sometimes be different. Let's focus on our commonality rather than our differences. You may agree to work on agenda Item A and B, but not C. Another group may want to focus on A and C. That's OK because there are plenty of issues where we can work together."

One participant suggested that the final report should include principles, a strategy, and suggestions for practical actions to deal with the problems. He thought the ideas presented in the report would gain broader acceptance if they are suggestive rather than dictatorial.

Another participant said we need to identify a unifying theme for **Children of 2010** so we can move above all of the disparate issues. He noted that group discussions about diversity can easily become sidetracked about specific, interrelated problems. In addition, the issues are so powerful and personal that it can be difficult for individuals to move beyond an expression of "my story." A successful response for **Children of 2010** will require an approach and theme that helps people move quickly to a strategic and comprehensive level of thinking.

One of the meeting leaders said that the next dialogue session would focus on successful action strategies that have broad applicability to the challenges of 2010. She quoted Horace Mann: "Be ashamed to die until you have won some victory for humanity."

Visions of 2010

Toward the conclusion of the session, participants shared their personal visions of 2010. Rather than seek a collaborative, universal statement, their task was to write, individually, a statement of what they personally hoped would come to pass for the children of 2010. Following are the notes that some participants chose to share with the meeting reporter:

- In 2010, children of all ages will be experiencing educational programs built on demographic principles that prepare people to participate/contribute to a true democratic society.

- In 2010, my nation will hold high expectations for every child, nurture and provide opportunity, teach each child through the strength they bring, respect each child and teach them to respect themselves, view every child as a valued contributor from the earliest ages, and have hope for the future.

- By 2010, the [organization where I work] will try to demonstrate how to re-build communities and transform neighborhoods to help give families the tools to raise their children in ways that give them the best chance to develop physically, socially, and intellectually and to succeed to the best of their potential.

- In 2010, my community, tribe, and family will not be victimized.

- In 2010, my nation will have revitalized the American democratic system so that our young people are no longer alienated from our political system, nor feel they must either beat or hustle the system, but use and change the system for the good of all.

- In 2010, my country will take responsibility and have respect for all its children, so that all necessary social supports to ensure the success of every child are in place.

- By 2010, the Hispanic community will be in a position of power and influence with our growing numbers and our great purchasing power (today it is $300 billion) if: (a) the family is supported with parenting and social support, (b) children have a strong early childhood education program, (c) schools are sensitive to the needs of our people [by] providing equitable educational opportunities, and (d) if those of use who broke the social/economic barriers provide the necessary support, mentoring, and opportunities. We will have a group of Hispanic leaders in the year 2010 who will join other young leaders from other ethnic groups to create a better nation and world where everyone is respected.

- In 2010, child advocates will face new challenges that we need to be prepared to meet but that we can't predict.
- In 2010, the organization where I work will organize an alumni [organization] of parents and graduates who will be politically empowered to help the program gain respect and expansion because of its richness of content, not because it serves low-income families.
- In 2010, I envision a social security system for children 5 and younger.
- In 2010, I will campaign for a woman of color running for President.
- As an optimist, I hope in 2010 the United States will be in the position of providing itself as a role model for a successful multiracial/multiethnic/multilingual community.

Reflecting

Some Things Will Never Change
by Geoffrey Canada

You can ponder with all your might
Spending a score of sleepless nights,
On matters of philosophy, theology, ecology.
And after doing all of that
You still cannot dispute the fact
That water runs downhill.
Some things will never change.

Why wish for clouds to disappear
Or pray for sunshine all the year?
Regardless if you think it best
The sun will always travel west.
Just face it.
Some things will never change.

Why mourn the evening's loss of light?
You know that daytime follows night.
Or beat your head against the wall
In anger that the leaves will fall
In time.
Some things will never change.

We check our stocks for highs and lows
Not the ticker tape of our souls.
Ignoring the most important fact
Not what we take in, but what we give back.
The clock is ticking.
There might be time for change.

Why should the accident of birth
Be a blessing to some, to some a curse?
Just hold an infant to your breast
You'll see one feels like all the rest.
Is there any reason for delay?
This we must change now, today.

Reprinted with permission.

Good Omen for the Future

On Thursday, June 8, 1996, approximately 500 Puyallup tribal members, friends and Chief Leschi School employees, witnessed a special blessing and raising of the Chief Leschi School story pole. Our pole is made of cedar and stands 36 feet high. It has been about 150 years since the Puyallup Tribe has raised a traditional story pole. The raising of our story poles represents the revival of our Native American arts and nearly forgotten traditions.

As the story pole was raised, a hawk and an eagle circled the sky above the pole, signifying a good omen of good things to come for the future. Speakers talked of days in the past when Native Americans were badly treated and assimilation was forced upon tribes. Today, there is hope that Native American children will be given the chance to freely express and maintain their heritage.

From the Web site www.leschi.bia.edu

More food for thought

Within weeks after the conclusion of the final dialogue, the White House released the final reports of the President's Initiative on Race. These documents provide additional information that may be useful for reflection. At the time *Children of 2010* was published, they were available for downloading from the Internet at a subdirectory of http://www.whitehouse.gov.

One America in the 21st Century: Forging a New Future[29] is the 229-page report of observations and recommendations. In support of the President's Initiative on Race, the Council of Economic Advisors published an 80-page companion volume: *Changing America: Indicators of Social and Economic Well Being by Race and Hispanic Origin.*[30] Statistical data from the Bureau of the Census, the Bureau of Labor Statistics, the National Center for Education Statistics, and other federal agencies are summarized in the Council's companion volume.

Dialoging about diversity and opportunity

There are so many issues to discuss! Cultural diversity, the implications of language, respect for individuality, fair access to opportunity, the economic implications of access, and the need for change are just a few of these. Some questions and issues to consider are below.

1. The Hispanic population encompasses both individuals born in the United States and immigrants. It includes people with cultural roots in such diverse nations as Chile, Cuba, El Salvador, Mexico, Puerto Rico, and the United States. Are we "stereotyping" people by lumping them together as Hispanics or Latino? On the other hand, what are the positive reasons for embracing the Hispanic identity?

2. What are the implications of using the category "Asian/Pacific Islander"? Does it make a difference that persons from Cambodia, China, Japan, Korea, the Philippines, and other Asian nations speak different languages?

3. When should schools communicate with children and parents in English . . . when in other languages?

4. Are non-Hispanic Whites with ancestries in Belgium, Greece, Ireland, Poland, and Russia all alike?

5. How do we achieve a balance between broad racial and cultural identities . . . and specific heritage and individuality?

6. Do schools in your community show respect to children and their parents—regardless of individual or cultural differences? Do early childhood programs, hospitals, and police departments?

7. If education is such a powerful determinant of economic and other outcomes, how do we make sure that our educational institutions give fair access to all children?

8. What resources and skills do children need to gain fair access to educational and other opportunities?

9. What is the economic fate of children who do not fare well in conventional school settings—because of individual differences, cultural/language barriers, or many other causes?

10. Are there alternatives to "educational tracking" of students, a practice that tends to route a disproportionate number of minorities away from a college education?

11. What are the implications of a disproportionate share of lower-income students being concentrated in community colleges, which tend to have lower retention and completion rates than "first track" institutions of higher education?

12. Persons who have a baccalaureate degree earn dramatically more, on average, than high school graduates. Does this mean that most adults in the United States would be affluent if 80% of them completed a baccalaureate program?

13. Is it more realistic for individuals to work for institutional change . . . or figure out how to "beat the system"?

14. What is your vision for making educational and career opportunities accessible to all of the children of 2010?

15. What racial and ethnic groups reside in your community? How can you involve them in your dialogue? What do participants from different groups think about the questions posed by this book?

Best Practices: Principles, Volunteerism, and the News Media

Focusing

Scope of the second dialogue session

Dialogue participants used the second session to explore practices that would promote a workable, inclusive democracy for all the children of 2010. Conducted on May 27 to 29, there were four themes:

- **Principles of best practices,** as important factors for building a good future for the next generaton

- **Volunteerism,** a best practice for giving children and youth experience in a participatory democracy

- **News media,** as a tool for advocacy and direct services for children

- **Movements,** as a means for promoting needed changes—the subject of the next chapter.

Rather than attempt to generate a catalog of specific programs and policies that exemplify aspects of "best practices," participants sought to identify the underlying principles that were universally applicable. To many attending the meeting, this seemed like the most difficult session. The group struggled with how to reconcile the suggestions of individual participants, who had divergent opinions—and even different ways of perceiving and talking about issues. In addition, one of the planners conceded that it was "difficult to get our arms around the concept of 2010 because there are so many variables–such as diversity, economics, worldwide trends, and other change."

Sharing a society where people are different

Even though diversity was not the session's central focus, the participants considered race and ethnicity a key consideration when envisioning a viable future for *all* children of 2010. The success of the civil rights movement was used as a possible analogy to the anticipated success of the proposed children's movement. This will be discussed in a later section.

Jim Vance, a presenter and news anchor from WNBC4 television station, hoped that 2010 would resemble his recollections of 1950, when he lived in a neighborhood he dubbed a "mini-United Nations." "My goodness! How little those differences mattered then," said Vance, who recalled neighbors coming from many different countries.

But in 1950, only the children were integrated. As a young child, Vance was welcome in the house of White children. But he never noticed that the parents of his White friends did not commingle with his African-American parents. By 1952, White families began to move to the suburbs and ethnic minorities formed enclaves. After 1955, Vance's diverse neighborhood had changed forever.

The children of 2010 do not need to live next door to different cultures to experience diversity, Vance said. But their society should reflect tolerance and respect of all cultures.

Although no one would have disagreed, the participants debated diversity's appropriate reach. The word "tribalism" was used for one extreme; at another point, "assimilationist" was used for the other extreme. Tribalism, said one, is healthful to an extent.

In discussing diversity, the dialogue participants ran the risk of seeing the issue as "either/or," said one participant. Either we have diversity and it is good, or we do not have diversity and it is bad. Instead, we might have diversity when it is advantageous, and we may form coteries when it is appropriate.

One participant observed that even the meeting divided into cliques, which would necessarily alienate some. Is this exclusion an example of what goes on in society? The participants decided that it was . . . but it exemplified a customary practice of natural camaraderie.

For the purposes of this conference, the participants were asked to answer a question: Who is working for inclusiveness on behalf of our children for 2010? The panel did not answer this question, but considered parental views an important factor to achieving this goal. The panel stressed the importance of helping non-minorities recognize the promotion of diversity as advantageous to all children.

Despite the merits of growing up with exposure to both diversity and one's unique cultural roots, the panelists implied that they should concentrate on universal benefits. One participant suggested that their movement should focus on what is good for all children.

Beyond diversity

Clearly, *diversity* was the focus of the first meeting in April. At the May session, one of the meeting planners requested that that focus become broader. "If we make diversity the main issue," he said, "I think we lose."

He acknowledged the effect an ever-more diversified society will have on the children of 2010. If demographics change, people and institutions will have to change. But our central focus is not diversity; it is how to improve the lives of all children of 2010.

One of the reasons for the shift in emphasis is that the group explored the possibility of initiating a movement for children. The movement should be inclusive and benefit all children. While there is not yet clarity about the scope and goals of this movement, participants provided a variety of suggestions and caveats.

Principles of best practices

Over the course of the discussions, participants reflected on "best practices." They proposed principles of best practices—guides to creating a better future for the children of 2010. Those identified are listed:

Youth participation. Young people should participate in creating their own future. How this is accomplished, however, needs to be accomplished with great care because of cultural differences among our young people and their families.

Civics. Schools need to place a greater emphasis on teaching civics—with real issues, rather than just facts about governmental structures. Moreover, they can gain an understanding of civics by having more opportunities to make decisions about their schools and other community institutions. Children need a practical sense of civics as a foundation for participating in a democracy.

Clarity of mission. A movement for the children of 2010 will need an understandable, clearly stated mission. A well-developed mission statement is a powerful tool.

Measurable outcomes. Bettering the future for our children and youth will require quantifiable goals. We want to move beyond rhetoric to results.

Resources. We need to expand our horizons regarding where we will obtain the resources to improve the future for the children of 2010. This includes exploring and making use of nonconventional resources.

Data/research. Our movement will need well-researched information. There are many misperceptions about the needs of children, youth and families. Moreover, empirically based data about outcomes will be needed for sound decisionmaking.

Inspirational story about the movement. Every movement needs an inspirational story about the origin of the movement—something to galvanize public opinion.

Identity/attachment to the movement. All Americans need to be able to relate to the movement.

Ability for self-knowledge. Understanding oneself is a necessary part of participating in a democracy, particularly in a nation of diverse peoples.

Ideologically inclusive. Achieving change means that we must be able to appeal to a very broad political spectrum.

Definition of threats to children. We need to be able to identify the threats to the wellbeing of children and the barriers to their full participation in our society.

Parent involvement and support. Parental empowerment needs to be a key component of the movement.

Mutuality of interests (relationships). Our strategy must produce win-win situations for Americans who are different.

Fairness. Policies and institutions must be fair in providing opportunities for all children and youth.

Participating in **Children of 2010** was hard work. We shared a learning process about demographics, diversity and ethnic populations, youth participation and empowerment, economics, recent social movements, and the influence of the mass media. We contributed our own experiences and viewpoints, but we also devoted much time to listening to other participants who sometimes have markedly diverse perspectives. A meeting co-planner challenged us to cast off our old minsets, rethink the paradigms for change that we have taken for granted, and to take a fresh look at solutions for 2010. Achieving a shared, collaborative vision requires much thought and reflection. The four-month process offers us an opportunity to outline a vision of how our children will indeed be able to work together and prosper in a *United* States.

Exploring volunteerism

The power of service

Juvenile courts sometimes mete out community service to young people. A judge participating in the session noted that required service has sometimes resulted in better school grades and improved self-esteem.

One promising practice is empowering children to make decisions, serve the community, work with people who are different, and take the initiative in the learning process. One means for accomplishing this is volunteerism among children and youth. Based on her years of research at Independent Sector, Dr. Virginia Hodgkinson presented a panorama of statistical highlights about adolescent volunteering behavior. More information is available in publicatins such as *Volunteering and Giving Among American Teenagers 12 to 17 Years of Age.*[31]

In general, all children are underestimated when it comes to their contribution to the rest of society. According to Hodgkinson, a majority of children under 18 do volunteer work. Some 13.3 million teens volunteer an average of 3.5 hours per week, totaling 2.4 billion hours of volunteer time. Hodgkinson estimates the dollar value of teen volunteerism at $7.7 billion.

In addition to the benefits for society, volunteerism also promotes positive self-images. Over 70 percent of teens reported that volunteering is important because it broadens their perspective and allows them to do something for a cause that is important.

Most children who volunteer had their first experience before they were 12. And such experience is a good indication of volunteer habits in later life. Unfortunately, most who don't volunteer as teens *won't* later on, Hodgkinson said. "If you're gonna get 'em," she warned, "you've gotta get 'em while they're young."

Parents as models of volunteerism

Teenagers were much more likely to volunteer if their parents did. Fewer than half of the children whose parents did not volunteer volunteered themselves. But over three-quarters of the teens volunteered if both their parents did. Also, because fathers are less likely to volunteer than mothers, over 88 percent of children whose fathers volunteered were volunteers themselves.

Getting connected

Teens reported that the most likely place to become connected with volunteer activities was through a religious organization. Schools provided the second most likely source of information. In addition, other voluntary organizations are a frequent source of information about volunteerism in general.

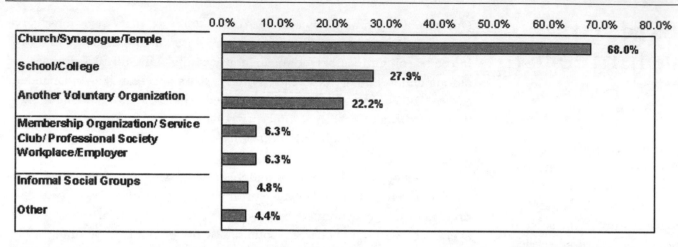

Virginia A. Hodgkinson, 1996. *Volunteering and Giving Among Teenagers 12 to 17 Years of Age.* Independent Sector, Washington, DC.

Figure 15. Organizations where teens first learned about their volunteer activities

Just ask

Hodgkinson stressed that people are far more likely to volunteer if they are *asked*.

• Of those who are asked, over 93 percent of teens volunteer
• Of those who are not asked, only 23 percent volunteer

The "asking" factor explained most of the variation between participants and non-participants. However, a troubling statistic is that African Americans and Hispanics are less likely to be asked to volunteer than Whites, as depicted in Figure 16. Of teen respondents, 54% of Whites were asked to volunteer, compared to 38% for African Americans and 45% for Hispanics. Yet, when asked, the overwhelming majority of Whites, African Americans and Hispanics reported that they actually volunteered (94%, 90%, and 85% respectively). Thus, a key to increasing minority participation in volunteerism may partly be a matter of *asking*.

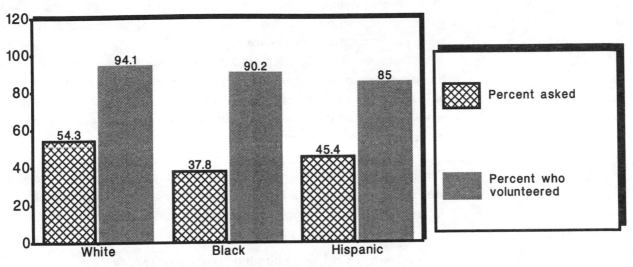

Figure 16. Percent of teens asked to volunteer and percent of those asked who did volunteer

Who are the people who ask teens to volunteer? Respondents to the 1996 survey said that friends asked them to volunteer 47% of the time. Teachers and other school personnel, family members, and people at a religious organization were also frequent askers. One tactic for broadening teen participation in volunteerism appears to be increasing the number of askers and encouraging them to be inclusive in asking everyone to volunteer.

Reasons

Teenagers have many reasons for volunteering, ranging from the idealistic—such as helping others—to the pragmatic—like enhancing their resume for college and job applications. They rated these reasons as "very important" for volunteering:

I feel compassion towards people in need. (84.1%)

I can do something for a cause that is important to me. (83.8%)

Volunteering allows me to gain a new perspective on things. (73.7%)

If I help others, then others will help me. (73%)

Volunteering is an important activity to the people I respect. (72.9%)

Volunteering will look good on my resume. (62.6%)

Most telling was the relationship between teens' personal goals and their volunteer behavior. Nearly 80 percent of those who considered "having a sense of belonging" a very important goal also volunteered. Given that

that sense of belonging is also a factor in joining gangs, teens' access to volunteer opportunities seems particularly important. Teens may fulfill their goals either positively or negatively.

Teens are also significantly more idealistic than adult counterparts; the same percentage volunteered of those teens who had an important goal of "making the world a better place." About 65 percent who had strong religious or spiritual commitments volunteered. Goals directly related to volunteering—for the sake of volunteering—factored less.

Other activities

Certain teen activities were associated with higher volunteer rates later in life, based on surveys of adults. (In parentheses is the percentage of those in each of these categories who volunteered later):

Working on a community project (91.3%)

Volunteer work at a church or synagogue (87.0%)

Going door-to-door to raise money for a cause (75.4%)

Tutoring someone having trouble in school (75.3%)

Loaning more than $100 to a relative or friend (73.2%)

Doing unpaid work (72.4%)

Developing the habit of volunteerism among children and youth is an important preparation for future social cohesion and problem-solving among 21st century adults, according to Hodgkinson, particularly if young people from all racial and ethnic groups participate in voluntary community service. In some cases, youth volunteerism can also provide exposure to working with people who are different—an affirmation that a diverse citizenry can be a *United* States.

Effects from volunteering behavior

Hodgkinson believes that volunteerism offers both personal and societal benefits. Based on national surveys, her teen respondents report multiple benefits:

Personal benefits

I learned to respect others (95.6%)

I learned to be helpful and kind (93.2%)

I learned how to get along with and relate to others (91.5%)

I gained satisfaction from helping others (90.2%)

I learned to understand people who are different from me (85.2%)

I explored or learned about career options (67.0%)

I did better in school/my grades improved (64.3%)

I've developed new career goals (61.6%)

Societal benefits

I understand more about good citizenship (83.3%)

I understand more about how voluntary organizations work (81.3%)

I'm more aware of programs in my community (70.1%)

I learned how to help solve community problems (59.4%)

I understand more about how government works (50.2%)

Teenagers perceive that they have plenty of reasons to volunteer. But again, they must have access to volunteer opportunities.

The teens had mixed feelings about "required volunteering," which some school districts enforce as a step to graduation; Hodgkinson does not support the concept. As the statistics show, however, they are likely to volunteer if they are simply asked.

The participants discussed the implications of these data. One questioned the assumption, a priori, that volunteerism is good. She asked: What about kids who don't feel there's anything to give back to?

This argument suggests that children in poverty or in an unstable family environment have too much to work out in their own lives to contribute to the betterment of others. A counterargument would propose that, in the process of helping others, youth are automatically helping themselves. This notion is reflected in a particular item within the teenagers' list of volunteer activities: Going through a personal crisis. An inference might be that interpersonal support and development was a solution to that crisis. As a result, youth volunteerism can serve to better both the people helped and the volunteers themselves.

This has implications for adults who volunteer for the sake of children. One panelist complained that this most often means adults doing something *to* children—tutoring, coaching, etc.—and not doing something *with* children. It is the rare project in which adults and children work together toward a solution, for a common goal. Most often, young people are treated as "objects, recipients, and resources."

But the panel cited instances in which children took a stand. Schools should teach children the value of becoming civic oriented, a participant said. The students should "learn that they can do something about a situation that is unfair."

Of course, the panel debated the definition of "unfair," and argued whether children could distinguish between that which was "fair" and that which was not. Certainly, a child could claim that having homework is "unfair" and thus refuse to do it. The job of adults is to identify when a situation is truly unfair and not simply something we do not want to do.

In an example of the former, a 5-year-old child noticed that a physically disabled peer did not have access to a handicapped parking space. Before long, the teacher helped her 5-year-old students organize a campaign for a handicapped parking space. The children's success stemmed from observing a situation that was unfair.

In another case, a group of West Coast first-graders learning about Washington, D.C., decided the city would be an interesting place to go. Their

Dangers of do-goodism

The initiatives of volunteers and other do-gooders can be a mixed blessing. One example cited at the sessions was a Native American community where outsiders wanted to solve the "problem" of only one well for water. After all, many residents had to lug the water a considerable distance to their homes.

So the White outsiders "helped" the community by drilling several additional wells. As a result, communication and community cohesion declined. After all, the communal well had been the singular location where residents shared news, gossip, and other information.

Notions such as volunteerism and "youth empowerment" might also have unexpected effects in some cultures. This is why any program initiative must be launched with great care and involve members of the community in the decisionmaking process.

intense interest and motivated fundraising efforts eventually turned into a four-day tour.

An initial reaction to these efforts is praise; here is living proof that children, with support, can get things done. The children are learning to participate in an activity that affects their lives. But as one panelist pointed out, the belief that children should be active participants in their own programs is not universal. It's okay to promote this participation. But in doing so, we should recognize that we are asking people to change their beliefs, possibly their culture.

Therefore, once we recognize a goal for our children's future, we should also account for diversity. Reaching that goal might require some degree of adaptation because the solution is the direct result of the methods. Agreement on those methods will most certainly vary from culture to culture.

A positive message to educate adults

Volunteerism may also "educate" adults about the many positive qualities of children and youth, including young people who are unfairly the targets of stereotypes. As an example, one participant compared African-American boys of different ages: the 4-year-old is "so cute," while the 6'2" 15-year-old with "baggy pants and a beeper in his pocket" is seen as a threat.

Adults are much more likely to respect and learn from that gangly teenager of color in a positive setting, such as that provided by volunteer activities. Not only is the teen volunteer accomplishing something for himself; he is letting the adult world know that "I am somebody, a contributor, an individual of value." This is a message that can reach out to adults who do not come into regular contact with young people.

Young minds and social betterment

The talents and energy of young people are essential elements for creating a viable United States for 2010 and beyond. As already noted, children and youth are idealistic. They are enthusiastic about the idea of making the world a better place and have much to contribute.

According to Virginia Hodgkinson's research, teens believe that specific actions can make a better America. Some of their ideas include corporations doing more to help the needy, rich people giving more of their money to the poor, getting people to work harder, and donating volunteer time. The ideas by percentage of survey responses are in Figure 17.

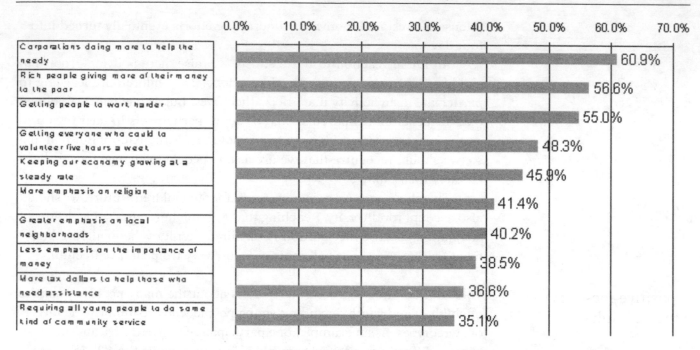

Virginia A. Hodgkinson, 1996. *Volunteering and Giving Among Teenagers 12 to 17 Years of Age*.
Independent Sector, Washington, DC.

Figure 17. Actions that teens believe would help a lot to make America better

News media: potential brokers for advocacy and change

We live in the Information Age, and it offers both problems and solutions for future children. While newspapers and interactive electronic media such as the Internet are important, television currently has the greatest media influence on our society, and our children. Thus, the dialogue sessions focused on TV—especially broadcast journalism because of its potential (and FCC-mandated responsibility) to serve the community.

Childhood past, present, and future

Jim Vance, anchor at NBC4, Washington's WRC-TV Channel 4, discussed his personal reflections about children of the future and the past from the perspective of his grandson, comparing the future to his own childhood. Vance used this as a starting point for reviewing the power television and its impact has on our society. He made suggestions about how a movement can work with the media. The text below is a paraphrase of his presentation.

Childhood Future

The year 2010 still seems somewhat remote to me. It is only 12 years away, but it has that 20 in front of it. It's a little like thinking of 50 when I was 35. I will not have any young children in 2010, but I do have a grandson who will be 14 in 2010. As it regards some of the more significant people in his life, my vision of his world, then, may not be all that utopian.

Take his parents, for example. Though they can hardly imagine it now, they will probably be working harder and longer hours than ever in 2010. The hardest work they may do is finding time for each other—and for him. Because of the pressures and expectations that they assume to be normal, they might be lucky to sit down together once a week, with enough time perhaps to have a lengthy conversation. Today, most of us find that finding time for each other is a daunting task, and I'm not sure it will be any easier in 12 years.

My grandson's teachers will probably be overworked, underpaid, and under-appreciated. That would be no change from the present.

His physician might seem faceless at times. For ordinary things, he may be diagnosed and treated over his home computer. And that treatment, of course, would be subject to the approval of an even more anonymous accountant at his parents' HMO.

He may have a hard time connecting with his preacher. People are finding less and less time for religion.

His grandparents will have left the area; gone to some new place in Capetown. They will see him on holidays and the occasional vacation breaks from school.

My vision of my grandson in 2010 is of a child who will have much more than I could have ever dreamed of as a child, especially as it regards access to information and opportunity.

I was 7 years old in 1949 when we got our first TV set, and I thought it was the most magical thing I would ever know in life. Imagine; you could even choose from three channels!

When my grandson turns 7, he will have 500 channels from which to choose on a digital screen bigger and clearer than life, and he'll take it for granted. What he will find on those 500 channels and to what extent they will enlarge or diminish his life is an important issue.

While my grandson and many other children of 2010 will have more and know more than you and I did as children, there will be some deprivation, too. They won't know it as such, but you and I will.

Childhood past

It is not likely that my grandson will know the joy or realize the benefits of growing up in a neighborhood like mine: a miniature United Nations. It was a working class neighborhood. My grandfather was a plumber. Across the street were the Sacchettis; they were bricklayers. Up the street were the Jagnesaks; sheetmetal workers. Four doors down, the Burns family; Irish carpenters. All of the families were large; my grandfather had 16 children.

Nobody had air conditioning, and walking through my neighborhood on a summer evening was a feast for the senses. All of the windows were open, as were the doors. You could hear the screen doors slam open and shut every two seconds, and out of those doors came all of the sights and smells of life.

A stroll down any street gave you witness to the loving and raging and whispering and shouting in what seemed like every language on earth. And the smells, O Lord, the smells of pasta, and cabbage, and goulash, and pork chops. Bread baking, and garlic, and onions, and greens. You could have just finished eating, but taking a stroll would make you hungry again. And that's what I did. I ate stewed chicken and dumplings at home, headed to Joe Murphy's house for what they had, and then finished up at Dominic Saccetti's house. It was indescribably wonderful, but it didn't last long.

By the time I was ten in 1952, it was all but gone. The Sacchettis had moved, as had the Burns, the Jagnesaks, and the Goldblatts. We still went to school together and played on the high school teams. But we did not play together on the same playground, nor did we hang out. And after 1955, I never ate a meal in their houses, and they never set foot in mine.

What I did not recognize as a small child is that, while we little kids were playing together and assuming it to be the most natural thing in the world, I never noticed that the grownups in my family—and the ones in theirs—never comingled as we kids did.

As we played in the streets, they sat on their separate porches and watched. As an 8-year-old, I was welcome in their houses; it never occurred to me that my parents weren't.

I remember those early years as truly the happiest time of my life. I knew a little something of at least five different languages. While I did have a sense of some differences among us, goodness, how little those differences mattered.

If there is anything my grandson is going to take for granted, how I wish it could be an experience like mine. Yet that may not be, and maybe that's OK. I am willing to accept that my early childhood was precious and peculiar. The tolerance and acceptance and appreciation for other people and other cultures that accrued from it stand me in good stead to this day.

A look at the media

Let's now look at my view of television and its relationship to what **Children of 2010** is attempting to do here today.

Despite change, my vision of the children of 2010 is not polluted by despair. I refuse to buy into the gloom of some of my peers whose prevailing notion is that society and our children are going to hell in the proverbial handbasket.

I have a brighter outlook about the future partly because of what I do for a living. The world is not going mad, and, especially, our kids are not going to ruin. However, we as casual consumers and viewers are not getting the whole story or the whole picture.

The word *casual* in regard to information consumers is important: The whole story is out there; the whole story is to be had. But it takes some work—more work and time than most of us are willing to commit.

Television is indeed a pervasive, important, and occasionally insidious force in our lives. Television stations and networks for the most part are profit-making entities, not public servants. They make lousy babysitters.

However, TV is not the bogeyman. It is not the source of ill in society, nor is it what's wrong with America today. It is not evil.

Television is an incredibly powerful tool that has yet to realize its potential for good, and it sometimes demonstrates an awesome capacity to do harm. Yet, there have been some wonderful moments on television. Who that saw it can ever forget the landing on the moon—live—right there in front of our eyes? Who saw Dr. King's speech on the steps of the Lincoln Memorial and didn't know instinctively that something momentous had just happened? Who watched that fateful encounter between Jack Ruby and Lee Harvey Oswald and wasn't awestruck by the devastating immediacy of the moment?

And who has watched Michael Jordan soar and glide and fly—and not been thrilled? Television has indeed elevated us, and it has disgraced us. Some of the "tell your dirt" talk shows on television disgrace everything that is decent in us. Every cutaway from regular programming for a live broadcast of yet another car chase on an L.A. freeway is an insult. And I, for one, feel sick every time I see the horrible spectacle that the media has made of highly-publicized court cases such as Whitewater.

Television has elevated us, disgraced us, and changed us.

Those images that came into our homes on a nightly basis from Vietnam were more than any administration or the national consciousness could tolerate. The pictures from Selma and Montgomery, from Philadelphia Mississippi, challenged our sense of ourselves to such a degree that we had to change. The work of Edward R. Murrow with migrant workers, and with Joe McCarthy, is legendary.

Television has touched us in marvelous ways, and time and again it brought out the best in us. Tens of thousands of people in the Saiiel region of Africa died before the gut-wrenching report from a British journalist moved our government and our people to stop the starvation. And the response to the victims of historic flooding in the Midwest a couple of years ago showed America and Americans at their best.

The reaction to the sextuplets in Iowa last year was wonderful, which brings up a dark side of television, of which I have personal knowledge and involvement. At my station, we played the Iowa sextuplets big, just as everybody else did—and properly so. However, as it happened, just days before the sextuplets, a local Washington-area couple enjoyed a multiple birth—also sextuplets though one of the infants died.

While the couple in Iowa was showered with congratulations and gifts and national celebrity, the local African American couple got barely a mention on any of the four local TV stations.

Every morning we meet to determine the day's coverage. The day after the hoopla in Iowa, the one Black person in news management, at that time, pointed out the obvious: We had ignored the local story, and perhaps the local parents and brand new babies might also need a little help. We then jumped all over the local story, as did the other Washington television stations.

Here now is where the value of diversity in the work place was borne out. There was nothing evil in the fact that we did not move on that story earlier. While I don't think there is a racist among them, management at our station—as in most television outlets—is predominately White, male, and middle class. Despite the best intentions, there is a different level of sensitivity and awareness when the workplace lacks diversity.

Our management was eager to correct the oversight, and this is not unusual or unique to our shop. Yet, it is not abnormal for a local, urban television station to jump all over the story of a missing blond-haired little girl in the suburbs, while regarding with somewhat less urgency the same situation involving a Black child in an inner city neighborhood. While the two reactions do not necessarily suggest racism on the part of news management, they do definitely require the sensitizing of that management, and the correction of clear and obvious diminution of one child in relation to another.

These are the kinds of issues we grapple with every day in television. Having spent a lot of years engaged in the struggle, I can tell you this: The people who run TV stations want to do the right thing, but we don't always know what that is—or how to do it. But we want to do the right thing, and it is important for you to know that we are open to suggestions.

Community outreach

Most of us do not set ourselves either above or apart from the people to whom we broadcast. In fact, some of us in television are reaching out to the communities, asking for direction and help. We don't ask for people to tell us how to do our job but rather to help us do it better.

Since the television set has become a popular family member in many homes across the nation, we creators of the content have to take our responsibility wisely, carefully and seriously. We do, and for two reasons: First, the television industry is a business, and we want to make sure that the children of 2010 are as good a customer then as their parents are now. The only way to do that is to serve their interests now so that they will continue to be viewers 10, 20, and 30 years from now.

Secondly, and more altruistically, we are all parents, family members, and citizens of this society. We want the best for our children, too. So like any good parent, we use the power of our office as best we can to make the world a better place.

NBC4 has taken a direct approach to our community service efforts. We created a mission statement for ourselves, and it is virtually the basis for everything we do at the station, for every piece of business we conduct, for everything that goes on the air. The essence of our mission statement is that we will "listen to the community to find innovative ways to meet its needs" to build a lasting trust with the people we serve.

In this interactive world, we've discovered that we also need to be interactive. We want to keep an open dialogue with our viewers, to know their wants and needs, and to understand what we can do to respond. We seek our viewers' counsel in neighborhood meetings, community boards, and open houses with all ethnic groups, religions, and people with special needs. One group on which we have placed a special focus is our children.

Over the past five years, we have undertaken a special effort to hear from children and from those who serve them. Based on what we've learned, we have created a huge station effort called "Working 4 Children." Its components are many, ranging from regularly scheduled positive news stories about young people who are doing spectacular things to special programs, both on and off the air, like conflict resolution and how to stay out of trouble.

We also sponsor events like the *Global Village*, a major free event on the Mall that is designed to educate kids about how people live around the world, particularly in third world countries. Over 40,000 kids attended that event, and others viewed our broadcast. People who saw it came away with a better understanding of the diversity of our world and what is good about diversity.

There are other things we do for kids with a more tangible outcome. *Camp 4 Kids* is a sponsored campaign that raises money to send to camp hundreds of children who could not otherwise afford it. *Just 4 One* is an employee-driven effort to adopt a graduating high school student and raise money to send that student to college. But, more than cash, we offer other kinds of support like internships, job training, and friendship. We have just graduated our first student, and we've signed our next one already!

I could go on with a list of impressive "Working 4 Children" projects, but I won't because bragging rights really are not the point here. What's important, as **Children of 2010** develops a strategy for the next generation, is to know that there are many organizations like ours that have the power to communicate important messages. And they are willing to do so. Partnerships with media organizations are a viable way to accomplish your goals.

Let us look again at the Global Village as an example. Andra, a non-profit organization, came to us with information on their global village project. Recognizing the value of their message, but also the value of our airtime, we were able to meet their needs and ours, while still serving the community. We created a three-way partnership, bringing in sponsors—advertisers who wanted to be associated with a project about kids and diversity. The advertisers underwrite commercials for the event, which we carry on our station. Everyone got their message across; the public was informed, and everybody won.

It is partnerships like these that can make the difference. Television has the unique power to bring people together in ways that we have yet to discover. Use it. Get to know it like you do the other members of your family and community. Like the kids do. You can find ways to make it work for you.

Group discussion about the media

Despite some positive trends in the media, the participants criticized certain aspects of media coverage. In particular, everyone was concerned about the coverage of children doing bad things. The recent school shooting in Oregon (as well as similar shootings in Mississippi, Kentucky and Arkansas) were covered because they were *news*, because they were abnormal, said Vance.

"News ain't what's normal," he added. "That kind of behavior is abnormal." That was why the media tried to balance such coverage with children doing "good" things.

No one disagreed that the public should know about a school shooting. But the panel pointed out a couple of flaws in the media hype surrounding the Oregon shooting. For one, children killing children is not an abnormality in some environments, such as certain inner-city neighborhoods. Because children of minority groups are more likely to inhabit those neighborhoods, the shooting by and of suburban White children would get more coverage than that of urban minority children.

Second, reporting only aberrations has the risk of avoiding the coverage of systemic issues. Because the recent school shootings were aberrations, the media's attempt to connect them to larger societal problems tended to fall flat. Instead, a participant suggested that the media focus more on those larger problems and less on the aberrations.

But more and more, the media are presenting children in a positive light. Some outlets are also making their own news through sponsorship of community projects. Vance cited newspaper-sponsored summer camps and Channel 4's "Global Village," a display on Washington's Mall that shows children how people live around the world.

Vance felt that social activists could still use television to make changes. The key is to let the media know that you really need them to get your point across, to promote your cause, or to encourage participation.

"It pays to be a pain in the butt," Vance suggested. "Keep coming back and keep coming back and keep coming back."

He cited an organizer of a youth basketball program who constantly left messages for the purveyors of local media outlets, including Vance. Such people shouldn't take no for an answer, he said, nor should they consider a brush-off the final word.

"Arrest your feelings," he said. "Don't take it personally . . . if you get rejected."

He also suggested that people who plan to use the media should get to know media representatives better. Find out the name of a station's news director or a newspaper's local news editor. Introduce yourself to them before you need them so they already know you when you do.

Though it takes effort to promote soft news stories, the media has become far more interested in them. He cited his own station's "Wednesday's Child" series—co-sponsored by Fannie Mae—that presents viewers with difficult-to-place adoptions.

"There's more that stations are willing to do about children's issues in the last five years," said Vance. "That's not going to change any time soon."

Reflecting

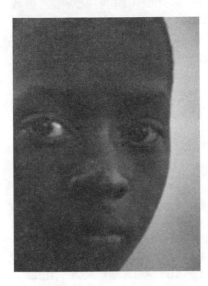

Young People Can Create Change!

Adapted from Barry Checkoway,
Young People Creating Community Change.[32]

Young people are solving problems and creating change, with a growing record of accomplishments. Here are some examples:

- Indianapolis youth are assessing needs and planning community improvement;
- Minneapolis youth are reaching out to gangs and challenging the forces of poverty;
- Detroit youth are serving meals in soup kitchens;
- New York youth are rehabilitating housing for homeless families;
- Selma youth are organizing against racial discrimination in the schools;
- Albuquerque youth are protesting against toxic wastes and environmental hazards;
- South Dakota youth are turning school classes into economic development; and
- Los Angeles youth are publishing their own citywide newspaper.

Characteristics of programs

Successful youth programs usually have a number of characteristics in common. First, they address problems that young people recognize as important issues for their community. Change-getting programs also help youth to organize and work together as a group. They encourage youth participation, multicultural collaboration, and youth leadership. Adults who assist the programs have learned to be allies without undercutting youth leadership or making all of the decisions.

Obstacles to change

There are obstacles to increasing the involvement of youth in community change. You should expect these obstacles as a normal part of the process and work to overcome them:

- Adults view youth as "problems" rather than as "resources."
- Adults plan programs without involving youth in the process.
- Adults do not share their power with young people.
- Young people do not view themselves as a group that can create change.
- Young people may have good ideas, but are unsure how to implement them.
- Young people are not organized enough for real influence.

A major obstacle to young people creating community change is *adultism*—the notion that adults are better than young people, and that they can control them without their agreement. The result is that adults may resist or oppose youth initiatives; and young people may question themselves, doubt their own abilities, and withdraw from participation.

Adults as allies

Despite adultism, some adults work closely with young people and become powerful allies in creating community change. These adults recognize youth as valuable resources with a right to participate and responsibility to serve the community. Such adults bring people together, provide resources for activities, deal with bureaucracies, and overcome the obstacles. They respect youth, give group encouragement, and build mutual support.

Starting with you!

Community change can begin with you. You can help youth take real problems, formulate some solutions, and organize with others to make a difference.

Reprinted with permission. W.K. Kellogg Foundation.

Citizens Escape Poverty To Reclaim 'American Dream'

by Lisbeth B. Schorr, author of *Common Purpose:*
Strengthening Families and Neighborhoods to Rebuild America[33]

Why, in the midst of a vibrant economy, are so many Americans still mired in concentrated poverty?

For Americans turned off on government, the answer long has been that nobody knows what to do about the great underclass maladies of joblessness, single-parent families, school failure, substance abuse and violence. In fact, we do know what to do on a small scale. Here and there, innovative programs have succeeded in changing life trajectories and setting children and families on the road to success.

The predicament is that successful programs are seldom sustained. When efforts are made to spread them, to bring them into the mainstream, they are strangled by red tape, rigid bureaucracies and archaic financing.

I set out in search of the people and places that had beaten the odds and had transformed not just a school but a school system, not just a social agency but a neighborhood, not just a few individuals but whole populations.

The secret of these successes? A few key people had the insight, courage and clout to climb out of old ruts and make fundamental changes on three fronts:

First, they achieved a new balance between flexibility at the front lines and accountability for the expenditure of public funds. We always have known that in the course of home visiting or providing prenatal care or even job training, people working on the front lines cannot be constrained by narrow protocols or circumscribed job descriptions. They must be able to respond, whether to a housing crisis or the need for child care or drug treatment.

What we now are learning is that if front-line professionals and agencies are to be able to do whatever it takes to help within mainstream systems, the systems must support their flexibility by judging them by their results rather than for their compliance with a maze of rules.

Second, successful efforts establish partnerships with citizens and community organizations that act more like families than bureaucracies. One national pioneer is Los Angeles County, which has contracted with 25 networks of grass-roots community organizations, including churches, Boys and Girls clubs and day care centers.

"These are the organizations," says Peter Digre, director of the county Department of Children and Family Services, "that breathe in and out with what's going on in the neighborhood" and are in the best position to be intensively involved with vulnerable families.

Similarly, to be effective, schools must be free to adopt coherent reforms, must be held accountable for student achievement rather than for compliance with the central office's ideas of how to teach and must allow parents and teachers to choose the schools within the public system that match their own convictions about the methods of education most likely to lead to successful learning.

Third, many successful initiatives have targeted an array of interventions on a single community to strengthen families and neighborhoods. Recognizing that narrowly defined interventions don't work for those in high risk circumstances, they are combining action in the economic, service, education and community-building domains to expand opportunity while strengthening individual capacity to respond to that opportunity. Empowerment zones and foundation-funded neighborhood transformation initiatives rely on a community's own strengths for designing and implementing change, while drawing on outside resources that bring clout and influence.

The evidence is there. From Los Angeles to Savannah, from the South Bronx to St. Louis, communities are taming bureaucracies, crafting new partnerships and putting together a critical mass of what works to transform entire neighborhoods.

We must act on what we now know to mobilize our resources, material, intellectual and spiritual, to ensure that all our children can grow up with a realistic expectation that they can participate in the American dream.

Reprinted with the permission of author.

Diverse Groups Tackle Community Problems

by William Bole, American News Service[34]

(ANS)—Opinion polls have shown what most people already knew: blacks and whites often clash in America, whether it's over O.J. Simpson or affirmative action hiring policies.

Beyond the national spotlight, however, a new surge of community activism is revealing another part of this picture. In a growing number of city neighborhoods and rural districts around the country, people are getting along—and getting things done—across racial lines.

For example:

• In Chattanooga, Tenn., black and white citizens sat down together for after-church brunches in restaurants and helped spark the city's cultural and economic revival.

• Not far away, in Memphis, black churches and white churches together hammered out a school reform agenda and got the city behind it—after having built the first community-based organization in the city where the Rev. Dr. Martin Luther King was assassinated three decades ago.

• In Hartford, Conn., gritty issues of urban life such as rat control and trash collection have produced an active alliance of residents from minority and white ethnic enclaves.

• In Sonoma County, Calif., Hispanic farmworkers and middle-class whites learned how to work together by fighting for each other's causes—from education to affordable housing—not just their own.

These and other initiatives have thrown light on what some regard as a new breed of civic organization, one that crosses the color line in forging grass-roots coalitions of common concern.

Many of the recruits in this movement—which has spread to all parts of the country—do not fit the popular activist stereotypes.

"We don't attract the Birkenstock liberals," said Mariba Karamoko, organizer of Shelby County Interfaith, an alliance of 48 Memphis congregations, half of them black, half of them white.

"These are people who haven't eaten a bit of tofu," he said. "They're middle of the roaders people who go to church every Sunday."

One of them is Ed Charbonnet, a computer analyst who got involved through his congregation, Holy Spirit Catholic Church, in white, affluent East Memphis. "I'm a card-carrying Republican. This is all new to me," he said.

Charbonnet was a leader in Shelby County Interfaith's successful drive for school-based management, or local control, and has pushed for new funds to repair rundown city schools.

He has also begun taking his daughter Clare, 12, along to meetings in black churches. "She really enjoys it. She gets very excited—'Daddy, when are we going again?'" Charbonnet said.

Citizens such as Charbonnet appear to be defying the odds at a time when polls show polarized black-white views of everything from the O.J. Simpson trials to public policy issues.

African Americans are three times more likely than the general population to see police brutality as a serious problem and are also far more likely to rate their local public schools as "only fair or poor" according to a survey taken last year by the Joint Center for Political and Economic Studies, a nonprofit research group in Washington.

"There has always been a wide gap between blacks and whites on critical issues," said Lee Daniels, spokesman for the National Urban League, based in New York. "The so-called racial divide is a fashionable phrase, but it's nothing new."

What's new, according to Daniels and other observers, is that ordinary black and white Americans are reaching for common ground in their communities, in apparently greater numbers than before.

"Those efforts are not reinforced by the larger society," he said. "There's very little notice given to them, and so you don't hear about them."

Behind some of the efforts are national networks such as the Industrial Areas Foundation, which organizes primarily among churches. Based in Chicago, the foundation counts 62 member organizations, representing congregations with more than 2.5 million families around the country.

The vast majority of the organizations are biracial or multiracial, according to Gerald Taylor, a national leader of the foundation who was the original organizer of Shelby County Interfaith.

Another network of this kind is the Pacific Institute for Community Organization, based in Oakland, Calif. Launched in 1972 as a regional coalition, the network has grown sixfold over the past decade.

It now represents 29 organizations, mostly church-based, in 60 cities as far east as Pensacola, Fla., and Brooklyn, N.Y., said the Rev. John Baumann, a Catholic priest who serves as the institute's executive director.

A key strategy of interracial organizations is to move beyond race by focusing on the shared interests of whites and blacks, along with those of other ethnic groups. "We organize around issues. That's the glue that holds people together," said Baumann.

It's not easy, though. In most places, bridging the racial gap means having to overcome deep suspicions and negative stereotypes, as well as vastly different perceptions of what ails the community, according to national leaders such as Baumann.

In Hartford, organizer Jim Boucher has seen Puerto Rican and Italian-American merchants slap each other on the back after winning a battle to keep city trash collection in their shopping districts. But he has also seen an accelerated process of white flight and urban decline.

"There's a lot of distress, and one (racial) group often blames the other group for things being so hard," said Boucher, whose organization is HART— Hartford Areas Rally Together. "It's a big obstacle to racial harmony."

Still, many are hopeful.

A little over a decade ago, Bessie J. Smith wanted to help make Chattanooga "one of the greatest mid-size cities in the United States," as she put it. So did a few hundred others who met over Sunday brunches that launched the citizens' movement Chattanooga Venture.

"We had white folks and black folks putting their heads together," said Smith, an 81-year-old activist from the historic black Erlinger section.

From these sessions emerged the ideas for a downtown aquarium and scenic river park—among other civic improvement projects that have become linchpins of Chattanooga's widely touted revival.

William Bole is Associate Editor of The American News Service. His articles have appeared in the *Washington Post, Los Angeles Times, St. Petersburg Times* and other newspapers and magazines.

The Value of Prevention

Dr. George W. Albee

Foreword to *Prevention: The Critical Need*[35] (1991) by Jack Pransky

Most people, if asked to rank order Albert Schweitzer, Mother Theresa, John Snow, and Ignatz Semmelweiss would put the first two names at the top and confess ignorance about the latter two. Yet in terms of contributions to humankind, like the number of lives saved, human anguish prevented, and accomplishments for the betterment of people throughout the world, Snow and Semmelweiss tower over the other two.

It may seem subversive, or mean spirited, to fail to praise Schweitzer and Theresa as recent-day saints, but I prefer the canonization of Snow and Semmelweiss.

As B.F. Skinner pointed out at his last public address at the APA Convention in Boston, Schweitzer was trying to save humanity one person at a time. Similarly, Mother Theresa, with a heart full of compassion and kindness, is also trying to save the world one person at a time. It simply can't be done. By way of contrast, John Snow figured out that cholera was a waterborn disease long before the noxious agent causing cholera had been identified. He observed that the pattern of cholera infection was related to where drinking water came from; in the most famous act in the history of public health he removed the handle from the Broad Street pump in London and stopped a cholera epidemic. Semmelweiss puzzled over the high rate of childbed fever and death in women in the public obstetrical wards of hospitals in Budapest. (In those days physicians didn't wash their hands, but wiped them dry on the lapels of their frock coats, so the more experienced physicians had stiffer and smellier coats!) Semmelweiss decided that somehow medical students and obstetrical trainees were carrying some unknown poison from the dissecting rooms of the anatomy lab to the women giving birth. He ordered all of his medical trainees to wash their hands for ten minutes before they delivered a baby. Suddenly and precipitously the rate of childbed fever and death dropped to almost zero.

The point here is that Snow's and Semmelweiss's work illustrates the truth to the dictum, "No mass disorder afflicting humankind has ever been eliminated or brought under control by attempts at treating the affected individual." These two public health saints have saved millions of lives, while Schweitzer, full of heart and compassion, was treating suffering individuals in his jungle hospital in Africa and while Mother Theresa was administering to the poor and hopeless in Calcutta. Individual treatment has no effect on incidence!

One cannot help but admire and respect those selfless people who reach out in humanitarian concern to support suffering individuals. But at the same time, if we respect evidence, efforts at prevention are even more humane and admirable if our criteria include the reduction of mass human suffering.

Reprinted with permission from Jack Pransky. Prevention: The Critical Need is available from NEHRI Publications, Cabot, VT. 802-563-2730

Dialoging about best practices

"Best practices" has a multitude of dimensions and issues, and dialogue participants focused on only a handful of these. Related questions and issues that serve as a discussion guide are below, but we also encourage you to identify and explore additional dimensions on your own.

1. In reviewing the *principles for best practices* developed by the dialogue participants, what would you add or delete from the list?

2. One of the meeting planners remarked that the central focus should be improving the lives of all the children of 2010, not diversity. Why do you think he said that? Do you agree?

3. Volunteerism was given as an example of a "best practice" for preparing youth to become actively involved in their community. What do you feel are the advantages and limitations of volunteerism in preparing youth for democracy?

4. What are the implications of lower participation rates for African American and Hispanic youth in volunteerism?

5. Do you believe that schools should make "community service" a graduation requirement?

6. Do you agree with Barry Checkoway (*Young People Creating Community Change*)—that young people can be responsible for action projects that cause change? Can you think of any examples of youth projects with which you are familiar?

7. George Albee discusses the value of prevention. Is it possible for our society to identify and prevent problems that the children of 2010 will otherwise face?

8. Jim Vance discussed the community service activities of a television station serving the Washington, D.C., community. What are the community services of news media in your community?

9. Have you, or someone you know, been successful in enlisting the news media for an issue or service that benefits children?

10. How could children's programs and advocates make better use of the media?

11. In addition to youth volunteerism and effective use of the media, what additional strategies would you like to discuss within the framework of "best practices"?

Best Practices: Movements to Change Society

Unquestionably, a better future for the children of 2010 requires social change. Embracing carefully-considered change, therefore, is itself a dimension of best practice.

In the second dialogue session, participants reviewed three movements that have affected social change in recent U.S. history. We intentionally focused on three case studies outside the arena of children's issues or civil rights. By so doing, we had an opportunity to learn from other movements—and explore whether there were successful methods that we could apply on behalf of the children of 2010.

In selecting the three movements, one of our criteria was that they must have changed the United States at the national, community, *and* individual levels. Second, these should be recent movements—preferably within the past 20 or 30 years. Third, they should demonstrate a large degree of success despite an initial lack of public consensus. Based on these criteria, we focused on the environmental movement, the antismoking movement, and the campaign against drunk driving.

This chapter includes brief case studies for each of these movements. However, we will first present our observations about the "successful practices" of a movement that can change society. After the case studies, we follow this book's format by including sections for reflecting and dialoging.

Successful practices of movements

A cause for commitment. Our three movements present the public with compelling causes for which millions of Americans are willing to commit their time, passion, financial support, identity, and energy.

Historic roots. Most movements for change have tapped into traditions that span more than a century, even when the contemporary activists have a focus or tactics that depart from that history.

Coalitions of interest groups. All three of the movements required the resources of many organizations and interest groups. The coalitions are often informal, rather than a structured "umbrella organization." Coalition members do not agree on all the specific issues or tactics, but they have often been able to work together on many strategic goals. Only through these coalitions do they assemble enough "critical mass" for causing broad changes in society.

Collaborative strategies. All three movements have prospered in part because of collaborative strategies that define attainable goals and action

tactics. During the Reagan years, for example, environmentalists formed the "Group of 10" mainline organizations to define a unified strategy to stop the administration from dismantling Clean Air Act provisions and other environmental legislation.

Clusters of issues. Movements generally have more than one issue or focus. The antismoking issues range from smokers to second-hand smoking, from targeting youth to risks for unborn children, and from health care costs to the targeting of Third World nations. Often, the organizations within the movement will focus on specific issues.

Alliances with other constituencies. Movements depend on alliances with other organizations who can provide channels for public education, lobbying, and action programs. The National Clean Air Coalition, set up in 1973, demonstrated the power of alliances between environmentalists and civic, religious, labor, and public health organizations.

Multi-level activity. The three movements are active at the national, state, and local levels—and their success depends in part on action at all levels. Some of the participating organizations are active primarily at only one level, but all levels of activity are necessary to achieve broad changes in society. Antismoking activists will target local enforcement of restrictions on the sale of tobacco to teenagers while also pressing for federal legislation and state antismoking policies.

Membership organizations. Movements include organizations with broad memberships, and this may be important for credibility, lobbying, and "volunteer power." Both Mothers Against Drunk Driving and the National Wildlife Federation, for example, each have 3 million members.

Core activists. Organizations within all three movements have a relatively small percentage of core activists who devote large, sustained amounts of time to the cause. Most are volunteers. Some organize groups, action, public education programs, media events, lobbying campaigns, and testimony at public hearings. Many do the important but unglamorous chores of preparing mailings, answering phones, and raising funds. By a "small core," we mean that a few thousand activists energize the movement with which millions of Americans identify. They also mobilize their less active members and sympathizers.

Simple summary messages. While there are a number of complex issues facing each movement, they have easy-to-understand "bottom line" messages for the public:

- People will get sick or die if we don't protect our food, water, and air.
- Don't drive if you drink.
- Smoking endangers nonsmokers.

A few outstanding leaders. Each movement has a few leaders who make a big difference. This may include serving as a spokesperson, ability to network, skill in building an organization, a knack for identifying the right issues and strategies, and an ability to organize resources. Some also have an encyclopedic knowledge of the facts, issues, and history of the movement.

Talented experts. Movements also gain talented experts who often contribute greatly to victories. They include attorneys, scientists, academicians, PR people, organizers, and fundraisers. Some of the best legal talent for the environmental movement emerged in the 1960s from late-night brainstorming sessions by Yale Law School students, including Richard Ayres, who became one of the founders of the Natural Resources Defense Council (NRDC) and senior attorney there.

Children and youth as change agents. All three movements have enlisted children and youth as change agents. A parent who fails to recycle or who smokes is likely to get persistent admonitions from the children. Schools and public service announcements are the most common channels for enlisting children.

Broad action. The movements encompass direct action, media events, public education campaigns, litigation, lobbying, factfinding, original research and technical reports, and sometimes services to victims. Some of the organizations within the movement will carry out special functions, such as the National Resources Defense Council—which deals with legal and legislative issues. Others spin off special-purpose activities, like the political action committee of the Sierra Club.

Galvanizing events. The movements tend to have a few galvanizing events that spark public concern and activism. In 1980, Mothers Against Drunk Driving was established, in part, because the 13-year-old child of a founder had been killed by a drunk who had prior offenses. During the 1960s, Cleveland's Cuyahoga River caught fire because it was overladen with pollutants. Sickness and death in the neighborhood of Love Canal (NY) informed Americans about the terrors of toxic wastes. For antismoking proponents, a galvanizing event was the 1964 report by the Surgeon General stating that cigarettes are a cause of lung cancer and chronic bronchitis.

Pivotal books. Movements may have one or several books that serve as the catalyst for broad public concern about a problem. Rachel Carson's *Silent Spring* shifted much of the focus of the environmental movement to public health issues and pollution.

Media exposure. The movements are proactive in gaining media exposure. This ranges from a presence on national broadcast programs like "60 Minutes" to community coverage of local accidents caused by drunk drivers or polluters. Very creative and effective tactics include the League of Conservation Voters' announcements of the 12 members of Congress with the worst voting record—dubbed the "Dirty Dozen."

"Bad citizen" publicity. The threat of negative publicity can cause change, because most businesses and governments do not want to be labeled as exploiters, polluters, or other types of bad citizens. Greenpeace tactics have caused many corporations to think twice about their business practices—simply out of fear of being targeted for direct action. Tobacco companies, once the beloved cash cows of Wall Street and Congress, are now pariahs.

Broad revenue base. The movements have a considerable funding base, with the environmental and antismoking movements each appearing to have revenues in excess of $100 million. Much of the funding is from individuals. Foundations also are important to financing movements. Grassroots groups raise revenues by selling memberships and asking for contributions—making them relatively impervious to any changes in priorities by government or foundation grantmakers. Government grants for public education about the environment, smoking, and drunk driving also play a complementary role, though these funds are often channeled through public schools and other mainline institutions.

Time. Successful movements seeking major changes in society take time, and the three studied here have required a minimum of 5 to 10 years to produce significant milestones at the national level. Thirty years may be a more realistic time frame for realizing the full benefits of major social change.

The environmental movement

The environmental movement has many dimensions. Issues range from wildlife protection and species diversity to acid rain, global warming, and chemical contamination of foods. Some of the groups are a century old; others are recent. They range from political moderates to those that are confrontational, including a few like Greenpeace who practice civil disobedience. While the overall movement counts many successes, the groups do not see eye-to-eye on a number of issues, resulting in some degree of tension. Mainstream players at the national level include the "Group of 10" who banded together to defend environmental laws during the Reagan years:

- The National Resources Defense Council
- Sierra Club (without tax-deductible status)
- Sierra Club Legal Defense Fund
- National Wildlife Federation
- Wilderness Society
- National Audubon Society
- Izaak Walton League
- Environmental Defense Fund
- Friends of the Earth
- National Parks and Conservation Association

History

The roots of environmentalism extend deep into the 19th century, reflecting the transcendental visions of Emerson and Thoreau. Some of the early practical applications were implemented by the Mormons who, faced with scarce water supply and influenced by the conservation practices of American Indians, adopted a community rather than "property rights" approach to natural resources. Much of America's early interest in environmentalism focused on the West—and stewardship of its wilderness and natural resources.

Social activism of the 1960s recast the environmental movement into a movement concerned about pollution and public health. Books like Rachel Carson's *Silent Spring* helped to transform the movement from an upper class endeavor of Audubonists and national park preservationists into a broader cause for middle class, primarily White, Americans. The surge in interest lead to a federal Environmental Protection Agency in 1970, both the ally and foe of environmental groups, depending on the specific issue or policy. The same year also marked the first Earth Day.

Environmental disasters also began commanding the public's attention. During the 1960s, pollution was so overwhelming that Cleveland's Cuyahoga River actually burned. The Love Canal neighborhood in New York state had been built on a toxic dump, and residents had a wildly high risk of becoming sick or dying. A reactor on Pennsylvania's Three Mile Island failed during the 1970s, giving Americans a taste of the potential for radiation poisoning. Smog in southern California had become legendary, underscored by a high incidence of respiratory and other health problems. The more radical environmental activists brought attention to other hazards, such as when Greenpeace plugged up the discharge pipes at a Dow Chemical Co. plant.

As time passed, the organizations in the environmental movement attempted to adapt to changing political and social climates. The Reagan years saw more of a defensive action—attempting to defend the environmental laws, regulations, and enforcement procedures already on the books. Belatedly, issues of environmental justice come to the center of the stage—issues facing racial and ethnic minorities like the exposure of migrant farm workers to pesticides, toxic dumps on "the wrong side of the tracks," and lead paint accessible to children in decaying housing.

Litigation

The contemporary environmental movement has a history of filing suits on behalf of environmental causes. The Natural Resources Defense Council (NRDC) was established in 1970 and modeled after the NAACP Legal Defense Fund. In its first year, NRDC found that many of the state plans for air quality standards failed to comply with the Clean Air Act of 1970. When EPA failed to force state compliance with the law, NRDC sued EPA and began winning.

Lobbying

NRDC borrowed the techniques of rivals in industry—sending experienced lobbyists to Congress, sponsoring original scientific research and reports, and using contacts within the Executive Branch to monitor shifts in administration policy. It also drafted key proposals for members of Congress. The political action committee of the Sierra Club spent $250,000 in the 1988 congressional races. Without the much larger budget and staffs of their industry opponents, they relied on public concern over environmental issues and positioned themselves as being part of the "just cause." They also formed broader coalitions with labor unions, churches, civic, and public health groups.

In many communities, local environmental groups are also active and vocal about many environmental issues. Public laws, enforcement, and private business practices often attract close scrutiny. Activists may be visible at public meetings and hearings, collect signatures for petitions, sign up residents as members, pass out fliers, and occasionally even picket offenders.

Public education

The national environmental groups have become skilled at media and public relations, capable of selecting the right issues for "60 Minutes" and other network programs. NRDC sold 110,000 copies of *For Our Kids' Sake*—with tips on how to protect children from pesticides in food—after Meryl Streep described the booklet on the Phil Donahue Show.

Some of the media attention is driven by environmental events. Two months after the Exxon Valdez oil spill, the Wilderness Society grew by 28,000 members (three times the normal monthly increase in 1988).

Much of the public education function occurs through other organizations that have made a commitment to the environmental movement, such as civic organizations, religious, labor, and youth organizations. Environmental education has become commonplace in elementary and secondary schools, with most of the financial support for these activities coming from local school district operating budgets.

Membership and revenues

The national environmental groups are membership organizations. According to information available in 1990, NRDC had 130,000 members, the Sierra Club had 550,000, and the National Wildlife Federation had 3 million. In that year, the Federation also had the largest budget—$85 million, while NRDC reported $16 million.

Sources for case study

Grossman, Mark. 1994, *The Environmental Movement*. ABC-CLIO American History Companions. ISBN 0-87436-732-8.

Weisskopf, Michael. April 19, 1990, "From Fringe to Political Mainstream, Environmentalists Set Policy Agenda," *The Washington Post*, page A1.

The antismoking movement

This movement highlights the rewards of long-term persistence. Society-changing victories came much more slowly than was the case for the environmentalists. Thirty-three years after the first shot in the modern anti-tobacco war, however, the fortunes of the tobacco industry are falling like the proverbial rock. Federal and state governments are asking for billion-dollar settlements, and selling cigarettes to teenagers is a crime.

Antismoking groups, public health organizations, consumer activists, and a few outspoken people in government joined forces to propel this movement to stunning victories in the 1990s. Action on Smoking and Health (ASH) is one of the oldest and most visible of the groups that focuses solely on this issue. Formed in 1967, ASH is engaged in legal action, public education, and defense of the rights of nonsmokers. The Center for Tobacco-Free Kids is the largest nongovernment group that focuses specifically on protecting children and youth.

Among large health organizations engaged in the movement are the American Lung Association, the American Heart Association, and the American Cancer Society. Ralph Nader's Public Citizen has been vocal as well. At the local level, there are numerous groups, some local chapters of national organizations, some with memorable names like GASP (Group to Alleviate Smoking Pollution).

The federal government has been a major player, though a reluctant one at first because of the powerful tobacco lobby and the former committee chairs in Congress who were from southern tobacco-producing states.

History

There have been antismoking sentiments ever since the noses of nonsmokers were accosted by wafts of tobacco fumes. Prior to the 20th century, there were efforts to make smoking illegal, and some people—even kings—complained loudly. While cigars were the mode for 19th century America, cigarettes emerged as the dominant product. They were marketed like candy, glamorized by Hollywood, and packaged in the military's C- and K-rations. Airlines gave away complimentary packets.

At the state and local level, activism to restrict smoking stretches back over a hundred years, but until recently tobacco was sacrosanct in Washington, D.C. In the 1960s and 1970s, however, the tide slowly began to turn. Savvy litigation and lobbying, the resources of national organizations, and long-suffering grass roots groups eventually changed the unchangeable.

For the war against smoking, the shot heard around the nation was the 1964 report of the Surgeon General, declaring that cigarette smoking was a cause of lung cancer and chronic bronchitis. In the same year, the Federal Trade Commission proposed adding warnings to cigarette packages, stating that they are "dangerous to health and may cause death from cancer and other diseases."

After pressure from industry, Congress intervened to protect cigarette makers. It passed the Federal Cigarette Labeling and Advertising Act of 1965, which authorized a weaker message but forbid the FTC or states from issuing any regulation that would otherwise interfere with tobacco advertising. With a resistant Congress, the antismoking battle moved in 1966 to the Federal Communications Commission (FCC), where John Banzhaf III—who a year later would found ASH—filed a complaint, arguing that radio and TV stations broadcasting cigarette commercials should be required to provide free time for the opposing, antismoking view. In 1967, FCC ruled that the "Fairness Doctrine" did apply to cigarette commercials, which would require the broadcast industry to run hundreds of millions of dollars of free antismoking messages.

For the tobacco industry, 1972 was a bad year. After years of fighting, the industry finally conceded to a ban on broadcast commercials. In the same year, the Supreme Court ruled that such a ban was constitutional. The

Civil Aviation Board proposed a rule mandating no-smoking sections on airplanes, and the Interstate Commerce Commission began considering a rule restricting smoking on interstate buses.

While winning some battles, the antismoking movement was not winning the war during the 1970s. The tobacco industry was doing just fine. Profits were good, and there were enough new customers to replace those who actually stopped smoking. The movement's strategists thought that lawmakers and agencies would "do the right thing" because they had overwhelming medical and research evidence on their side. Wrong. Regardless of evidence, the balance of power was overwhelmingly tilted in favor of tobacco. Industry bankrolled political candidates, research, expert testimony, and PR.

Grassroots rebellion

During the 1980s, some of the momentum for the movement came from the grassroots level. Maybe it was the positive side of the "me generation," or perhaps assertiveness training, or a growing interest in personal health. Millions of nonsmokers got mad as hell and said they weren't going to take it anymore. "Thank you for not smoking" signs popped up in offices and elsewhere. Many of the efforts were amateurish, but armies of children marched home and bugged their parents to stop smoking, often breaking the cigarettes and appealing to love. It became OK to tell smokers to snuff it in restaurants and other public places.

In 1981, the American Heart Association, the American Cancer Society, and the American Lung Association formed an antismoking alliance, the Coalition on Smoking or Health. They succeeded in gaining small victories like placing multiple warning labels on cigarettes, restricting smoking on commercial airliners, and gaining a small tax increase on packs of cigarettes. Later, the movement was aided by Surgeons General C. Everett Koop and Antonia C. Novello, who attacked secondhand smoke, nicotine's addictiveness, and advertising aimed at children.

By the 1990s, smoking had become about as glamorous as spitting in public, despite the tobacco industry's efforts at counterinsurgence, using tactics like Joe Camel, smoky stars in Hollywood, and big bucks for political campaigns. Beginning with the Bush administration, federal regulatory agencies stepped up their attack on smoking. EPA issued a report stating that secondhand smoke causes 3,000 lung cancer deaths each year, concluding that it was a "Class A" carcinogen like asbestos, arsenic, and benzene. OSHA and FDA began exploring antismoking options. With the Clinton Administration, the White House itself became directly involved, speaking out against teenage smoking.

Litigation

Early legal successes were state and local ordinances restricting smoking. At the federal level, early victories were primarily through regulatory bodies like the Federal Communications Commission, the Civil Aviation Board, and the Interstate Commerce Commission. Early attempts to sue industry for the deaths of smokers foundered against the fortress of tobacco's legal resources. A more recent tactic has been to seek court orders for closely-guarded industry documents, which indeed provide evidence that industry conspired to mislead the public about the health risks, increase addiction levels of existing smokers, and entice youth as new customers.

Once the cheerleader for a strong tobacco industry, the federal government has been pursuing a national tobacco settlement that curbs marketing to youth and provides some legal protections to cigarette makers in exchange for a $368 billion settlement. State attorneys general have also come to the forefront, demanding billions of dollars.

Lobbying

Tobacco allies no longer control Congress, and this has been an important element in the movement's current success stories. Of course, given the shifts in public opinion, it has become relatively easy for congressional leaders (in non-tobacco-producing states) to oppose the tobacco industry. Even political contributions from industry are less appealing, given the potential for wrath among antismoking constituents, who may monitor sources of campaign funds.

For the movement, one of the challenges is where to draw the line, where to compromise. Some of the more militant groups—reportedly the American Lung Association and Public Citizen—want no compromise and no legal protection for industry. Other groups in the movement, who are part of a coalition known as ENACT, believe that some compromise will be necessary to achieve sweeping antismoking measures that will reduce the chances of tobacco addiction among the next generation.

Activism

Many grassroots organizations have been involved in the movement. The Advocacy Institute, a Washington-based nonprofit that promotes activism for many issues, was one of the supporters of local antismoking groups. It took advantage of technology by using its electronic bulletin board to disseminate instant news flashes. According to some activists, electronic communications also enabled local groups to detect patterns in tobacco industry tactics that might have eluded them. Communication through the bulletin board became so important that American Tobacco Co. sued in 1994 to gain access to the network.

Personal computers and fax machines are now essential tools of community activism, enabling local groups to work together, share information, and coordinate activities.

Sources for case study

Action on Smoking and Health, Web site as of April 28, 1998, http://ash.org.

Encyberpedia, Web site as of May 1, 1998; Smoking medical reference information, www.smoked.com/

Schwartz, John. May 29, 1994, Smoking recast: from sophistication to sin; once-sacrosanct industry feels effects of grass-roots movement, *The Washington Post,* page A1.

Weinstein, Henry, and Levin, Myron. December 15, 1997; Smoking foes split as factions oppose industry immunity; health: as congressional battle looms, groups struggle over how to gain passage of proposed $368.5 billion settlement. Fissure may threaten the deal, some day. *The Los Angeles Times.*

The movement against drunk driving

The campaign against drunk driving is the most recent of the three movements considered here. In 1980, Mothers Against Drunk Driving (MADD) transformed a law enforcement and highway safety problem into a movement. MADD was formed after a 13-year-old girl was killed by a drunk driver who had prior offenses, and chapters were quickly organized in other communities. Offshoots from MADD are Students Against Drunk Driving (SADD) and Campaign Against Drunk Driving (CADD).

Unlike the environmental and antismoking groups, this movement has not had a history of suing the federal government. Indeed, anti-drunk-driving activists usually work in partnership with law enforcement and highway traffic safety officials. The National Commission Against Drunk Driving (NCADD), the umbrella nonprofit, includes both public and private leaders. NCADD is the successor to the Presidential Commission on Drunk Driving, appointed by Ronald Reagan in 1982.

History

The movement is partly an outgrowth of the temperance and prohibition movements, according to some accounts. During the 1800s, Americans became concerned about the domestic violence and lost worker productivity associated with alcohol abuse. By the 20th century, admonitions for moderation or abstinence evolved into a call for prohibition of all alcohol production in the United States. Such a ban was ratified in 1919 and repealed in 1933.

In addition, the movement is partly rooted in public concern about safe highways and automobiles. Beginning in 1965, Ralph Nader's *Unsafe at Any Speed* focused national attention on weaknesses in auto design and production. At the same time, there was great concern that more people were dying in alcohol-related car crashes than, annually, in the Vietnam war. Congress created the National Highway Traffic Safety Administration in 1970.

Individuals charged or convicted of drunk driving are in the hands of the judicial system. Prior to recent activism, courts often diverted drunk drivers into education and treatment programs without meting out sanctions. At the time, many courts saw drunk driving as a social and health problem, rather than a serious criminal offense. And media portrayed drunks as comical and lovable.

A basic tenant of the movement is that driving under the influence (DUI) is a crime and should be treated as such. Many in the movement, including MADD, set early goals of mandatory jail for repeat offenders, a higher legal drinking age, limits on the sale of cut-price drinks, and rights for DUI victims. Later goals encompassed lower legal limits for blood alcohol content, impairment by other drugs, and "designated driver" programs. MADD also seeks to build anti-DUI sentiment so that drunk driving is socially unacceptable behavior.

In 1990, MADD adopted a goal of reducing the proportion of traffic fatalities involving alcohol from 50% to 40% by the year 2000.

Lobbying and advocacy

MADD has been prolific in promoting legislation including more than 1,250 tougher DUI laws and 1,000 laws affecting victim rights. It has successfully advocated changes in federal laws as well.

MADD collaborates with federal and state officials to "Rate the States" on state progress in implementing and improving action against drunk driving. Ratings have sometimes prompted legislatures to move more speedily on laws and governors to improve programs.

In 1990, MADD also launched legislative proposals for victim compensation, dramshop liability, barring DUIs from discharging liabilities through bankruptcy laws, sanctions for child endangerment, and a constitutional amendment for victim rights.

Crisis organizing

Some community chapters of MADD have been organized in the aftermath of a tragedy involving alcohol-related fatalities. The accident becomes a focal point for galvanizing community commitment to tougher law enforcement, adjudication, and ordinances.

Public education

> "MADD had such a tremendous impact because MADD gave the issue a face and it gave it tears," said Belluschi, 48, who was severely injured at age 15 when a drunken driver smashed into her father's car. Arguably one of the most powerful citizen groups in the country, MADD has successfully lobbied for more than 2,200 pieces of state and federal legislation, including a drinking age of 21 and stiffer penalties for drunken drivers.
>
> —Robin Estrin, Associated Press.

Red ribbons attached to vehicles, reminding the public not to drive after drinking, are one of the most visible public awareness campaigns of MADD. An annual poster and essay contest involves thousands of school-age children. National Sobriety Checkpoint Week is a joint effort of MADD, law enforcement agencies, and corporate sponsors—drawing public attention to the high-risk travel period surrounding July 4th.

Much of MADD's public education strategy has been media oriented and at the community level. Media exposure is usually above average, because both the issues and MADD spokespersons are local. In many cases, the focus is on "hard news," such as a public policy, an accident, or a court case.

Victim support

The campaign against drunk driving is the only one of our three selected movements that seeks to provide direct support for victims. When victims approach MADD for help, a victim advocate will help the family prepare the victim impact statement, so the jury can determine how the victim's life has been affected by the drunk driver. The advocate will go with the victim to court, invite the victim to a support group, and help them apply for state victim compensation funds.

Outcomes

Alcohol involvement in traffic fatalities has fallen from 59% in 1980 to 42% in 1994.

Sources for case study

Brown, Beckie and Russell, Anne. (no date on Web page, accessed on April 29, 1998), MADD and Traffic Safety: Grass-roots Success

Estrin, Robin. Associated Press, August 6, 1997; MADD becoming victim of its success, *The Philadelphia Inquirer.*

International Association of Chiefs of Police, (Web edition undated), The Highway Safety Desk Book, www.nhtsa.dot.gov/.

University of Omaha, (no date on Web page), Prohibition Then; MADD Today, http:// ecedweb.unomaha.edu/lessons/feusA.htm.

Reflecting

A Man of Consequence

by Mary McGrory

Publication of Rep. John Lewis's autobiography, "Walking With the Wind," is a literary event, for sure. This is the definitive account of the civil rights movement, written in the first person by one of its leaders. It is also a political event. Lewis, a Democrat from Georgia, is universally regarded as a home run of a human being—brave, honest, humble. Now with the help of a skillful collaborator, Michael D'Orso, he has produced a compelling history that promises to become a sensation. . . .

. . . "Walking With the Wind" reminds all interested parties of just who was at the barricades in Montgomery, Birmingham and Selma. He fingers the peacocks and the poseurs. He even faults his idol, King, for joining demonstrations late or ducking out early.

Lewis, one of 10 children of an Alabama sharecropper, was born with a voracious appetite for justice and education. When the rest of the family went off to the fields to pick cotton, he would hide under the porch and wait for the bus he took to the wretched one-room school that Pike County provided for black children. He struggled to get into college, American Baptist Theological School, where he fell upon the ideas of nonviolence and joined the young lions from other colleges who felt that they were owed the right to be treated like American citizens—and, for openers, to be allowed to eat at public lunch counters.

On Feb. 12, 1960, they began the sit-ins that changed the South. The ensuing years brought Lewis an unremitting diet of violence and hatred from uniformed fellow Americans. He was slammed around without mercy by sheriffs, herded into paddy wagons with electric prods, flung onto jail-house floors, shoved, kicked and beaten. His skull was pounded by club-wielding state troopers and finally fractured in Selma, where unarmed demonstrators, including children, were set upon by their local police. Lewis recounts all of this in meticulous detail, so vividly that you read it as if you had never heard it before. He even tells you the kind of tear gas that Sheriff Jim Clark chose for the assault at Selma. In an interview the other day in his office, Lewis said he has just about total recall of the events. "I can remember what people said and when things happened—a beating in Montgomery, the reporters who risked their lives to witness."

The initial reaction to his book has been emotional. Last weekend at the Atlanta Historical Center, he was greeted by a crowd of 400. Among them was a white woman who, with tears streaming down her cheeks, called out: "Thank God you're still alive. We lost Martin Luther King and Bobby Kennedy, but we have you."

It is impossible to read this inspirational and hideous story of courage and cruelty without being moved. Blacks will read it with rage and pride. The civil rights movement was rife with idealism and good strategy. Lewis and James Bevel and Diane Nash and his other comrades were schooled in Christian doctrine and the Gandhian philosophy of nonviolence. They showed major self-discipline. In the early, almost idyllic days of the sit-ins, the members of Student Nonviolent Coordinating Committee (of which Lewis eventually became chairman), created a political movement that was a model of political activism. Everything was seen to: dress code, food, transportation, attitude. They walked in silence, they had one spokesman, they hung in. They won. There is no trace of them today. Maybe Lewis can revive in them that hope and faith, maybe at least persuade them to come out and vote again.

If there is one thing this splendid, pulsing book is saying, it is that anything is possible if you insist. John Lewis wasn't supposed to be in Congress. He was supposed to lose to Julian Bond, who was taller, lighter-skinned and nationally famous. But he's finishing his 12th year in the House, and he's a figure of consequence. Now that he has told his glorious, harrowing story, he will be even more so.

Dialoging about change

In achieving needed change for the children of 2010, there are many issues to consider. The case studies about movements do not provide easy answers. Rather, they are challenges to consider issues, grapple with questions, and explore how to apply the experience of other movements to action for children and youth.

Distinctions

We cannot simply clone other movements, because there is not a perfect fit:

- From its inception, any movement for the children of 2010 must necessarily involve a broad range of racial and ethnic groups. This has not always been the case in the environmental and other movements.
- Much of the work of the three movements in the case studies occurred in the context of a Democratic Congress and a Republication administration. This is currently not the case.
- Compared to 20 years ago, the average voter is older.
- Network television does not dominate the media as pervasively as it did 20 or even 10 years ago.
- New technologies, such as the Internet, are affecting the ways in which movements organize and communicate.
- The movements in the case studies were supported by activists who were more homogeneous, demographically, than the constituency we envision.
- Compared to antismoking and environmental move-

ments, "the enemy" is more difficult to target (i.e., no big tobacco industry, no big polluter).

Now that we have made distinctions between the movements in the case studies and action for children, here are questions for further dialogue:

1. What do you want to change?
2. What are you for? What are you against?
3. What do we hope to accomplish by 2010? By 2020?
4. How would you explain your movement on national television . . . in 10 words or less?
5. Why is your movement so compelling that the general public (non-parents, non-teachers, and non-experts) would commit major time, money, energy, and identity?
6. How would you transform into activists those adults who currently do not have regular contact with children?
7. Who is already doing major things for children and youth at the national, regional, and local levels?
8. What existing resources are there at the national level for litigation, lobbying, media relations, public education, research, inter-organizational coordination?
9. What resources are there for grassroots activism?
10. What roles might different organizations play?
11. How do you enlist activists?
12. How do you raise money?
13. How will your efforts make a tangible difference in the life of *each* child of 2010.

Visions of 2010
and How to Get There

Focusing

At the third and final dialogue session, participants achieved a sense of closure to their task of exploring and visioning the future for the children of 2010. The group recognized that the job of creating a better future for children still lay ahead and the dialogue activities were simply a prelude. For participants, however, that step was a very large stride in terms of exploring the many dimensions of the future, challenging old assumptions and strategies, and crystallizing fresh thinking about necessary action.

Participants recognized that an America bound by a unifying vision of hope and democracy will be viable for the children of 2010 only if we make access to opportunity fairer and more accessible. Focusing on "Visioning and Generating a Common Will to Change," the session was the last of three—exploring how the future American population, characterized by increasing racial and ethnic diversity, can live, learn, work, and prosper together. The session examined how advocacy for children can become more effective, cooperative partnerships with the media can improve the lives of children, the urgency of school reform and access to a good education, and the problem of violence by and against youth. At the session, the participants also shared their reflections and suggestions about a vision for the future.

As one meeting planner put it, "This process has neither a beginning nor an ending." Many before us have contributed to the well-being of children. Many others will continue to advance the cause of fair opportunity and healthy development for all children.

The third session featured presentations by three guest speakers: Joan Lombardi, Deputy Assistant Secretary for Policy and External Affairs in the Administration for Children and Families, U.S. Department of Health and

Human Services; Barbara Harrison, news co-anchor at NBC4 and a media representative who is active on behalf of children; and Geoffrey Canada, President of Rheedlen Centers for Children and Families in New York City. Their contributions to the session are interspersed with the overall discussions of participants.

Facts are just the beginning

Reviewing the first session in April, one of the conference planners remarked "We have discovered that facts are just the beginning. What we do with the facts are more important." Regarding the second session, she observed that "There are many promising programs. We can draw upon this portfolio of experience and practices to improve the lives of children."

"What remains is to examine our commitment to the next generation. As Horace Mann challenged us, 'Be ashamed to die until you win some victory for humanity.' What is it that we want to change, and of what will we be ashamed if it is still a problem in 2010?"

She also challenged the group to look beyond appearances. "My daughter [a teenager of color] attended a hip-hop concert this summer, and there were many, many upper-middle-class White kids there. At a superficial level, this reflects diversity and a degree of intercultural sharing, but I wonder how much it means after these kids go back to their mostly all-White suburbs. There is certainly little sharing and interaction at the deeper levels of community."

In the spirit of challenging our commitment, one of the participants said "We haven't really talked about people who don't make it, who don't respond to available opportunities." Simply introducing opportunities may not be enough, especially if they are not truly accessible to all children.

A future worthy of our children

Building a future worthy of our children depends on what all of us do in our families, workplaces, communities, and nations. We do that every day, I know, but now we will be able to reflect on our past and count the blessings we enjoy as citizens of a free and democratic country. I hope we will all be inspired to give our own gifts to the future, whether by helping to build a new park, cleaning up a river, restoring an old theater, raising money for a library, saving family papers and photographs, encouraging children to interview their grandparents, volunteering in our communities—all of these are measures of ourselves as citizens in a democracy.

—Hillary Rodham Clinton, at the White House Millennium Event

"The meetings have been a microcosm of the discussions that our society needs," reflected the session's moderator. "We need to broaden the conversation. How do we involve others?"

Another participant concurred. "The group's insights will not be effective unless we involve other people. How do we establish a vision of moral consensus—so we can move ahead? We need to begin articulating a moral vision of the future for children."

Reflection on themes of the previous sessions

The group reflected on the themes that had emerged during the previous sessions. Based on these, the group recognized a need to

Bring the discussion about the Children of 2010 to other groups. We need to bring dialogues about the future of our children to others, including ethnic communities, parents, people we work with, and others. It is particularly important that we reach out to people at the community level.

Challenge our vocabulary, our assumptions, and the status quo. As change agents, we need to continually take a fresh look at the possibilities and reinvent our thinking. The social and economic context, adults, and children all change; and we must constantly make sure that our ideas and practices match current reality.

Express a sense of urgency. Because we care about children, we must pursue needed changes with a sense of urgency. Based on our discussions, we understand that we must make the best possible use of our time, because improvements to conditions do not occur quickly or easily. Making a better world for the children of 2010 will demand a decade of focused, ongoing work.

Apply intergenerational strategies. Many of those providing leadership for organizations concerned with children and youth are older, and we need to consider how to involve the next generation on committees, boards, and other leadership positions.

Build values. While improving the cognitive skills of children is important, it seems to be emphasized so pervasively that other, equally important goals of human development are excluded. Values, for example, are pivotal to the healthy development of children. We need to place more of an emphasis on values.

Build institutions that help children and families. We need to rebuild and reinvigorate our institutions that serve children and families. Because of a variety of problems—inappropriate practices or outdated strategies, scarcity of money, faltering leadership, inability to respond to changing demographics, or other causes—many of our institutions are in-adequate. Just as surely as we need to rebuild the physical infrastructure of communities, such as roads and bridges, we also need to refurbish or re-construct the social infrastructure that serves our youngest residents.

Keep learning and remain hopeful. We are becoming a force for change, and we are gradually making a difference. We need to keep working together. We will continue learning from our experiences and will need to be open to change ourselves as we learn.

Developing a vision

"Children need relationships," Joan Lombardi emphasized. Parents, teach-ers, and caregivers must be at the heart of these relationships, but Lombardi extended the concept to encompass nature, technology, diversity, and the media. She said:

- Technology, especially how we work with information and knowledge is transforming society. It is important that none of our children be left behind.

- While technology is a major focus for concern, we must involve our kids with *nature*. Reconnecting with earth—the forests, plants, animals, and natural phenomenon surrounding our lifespace—is vital to understand-ing and respecting both our local and global communities.

- Heterogeneous families—those involving persons from several differ-ent cultures—are part of our future. This adds a new dimension to inclusiveness.

- A goal for ourselves and our children will be to appreciate our own cul-ture *and* to also have the grounding to move between cultures. These dual capabilities will enable us, and our children, to participate fully in the diverse future of our democracy.

- We should be ashamed about what is happening in the media–the sex and violence. Why have we been afraid to speak out? Our children de-serve a far more affirming and nurturing culture. We must express our outrage openly and vigorously.

- We need to reach our young people who are alienated. Far too many do not vote, do not get involved, and do not participate in their com-munities. They do not think they can make a difference. It is up to us to involve them, to demonstrate through more positive experiences that they can make a difference. The future of our democracy relies on their involvement.

Kids need relationships. This begins with parents connecting in genuine ways with their children. Additionally, there are also huge intergenerational issues, such as adult communities where older people are segregated from children and youth.

"The early childhood field is too quiet about the future," Lombardi said. "People seem to be afraid to step forward and speak out. We need to let people know they have permission to speak out.

"If we don't express our vision, other people—those with whom we may disagree—will articulate their vision and dominate the discussion."

Homework

Lombardi also challenged participants to take the discussion and action back to home communities. "There is too much emphasis on taking action in Washington. There also needs to be much more action at the local level." She also noted that speaking out once isn't enough. "We have to say things over and over."

One participant noted that community activism does not always focus on children. "People *are* active," she said, "but their issues do not necessarily benefit children." She cited issues like neighborhood parking stickers and exclusionary communities. We cannot assume that community involvement will automatically address the needs of children.

"We need to focus more on community issues, rather than simply promoting a national agenda," agreed another participant. "Stimulating and activating people requires that we support *their* concerns." He recounted the concern of a woman in Texas who was angered because a high-traffic roadway was being planned for construction in front of the local school. She wanted to go before the city council and propose changes but didn't have any experience in carrying out that kind of activism. "We need to tie into local, specific issues like this one, rather than just articulate a set of principles," he said. Local concerns are what energize movements and causes. A specific issue gives community residents the meaningful cause around which they can rally.

"In our community, we gain involvement by working directly with parents and other adults," said a participant from Texas. "We ask them to think about the risks and problems that children face. Then we ask them to form an image of healthy kids—how they hope and dream their children will develop." When they kindle this positive vision about healthy kids in an affirming community, they will work together for change.

One of the meeting planners observed that, in our lack of specificity to community issues, "we may be losing our goals to billboards. While we speak in broad, wordy, abstract statements, groups with other viewpoints are reducing local issues to slogans, scare messages, and visual images that can be communicated in five seconds or less.

"We are too wedded to the printed word," she added. "Our messages need to be more visual. Devotion to reading is a cult among our peers, but this habit is not shared by the general public. Today, people are making decisions based on video clips, sound bytes, and billboards."

Working toward cooperation and alliances

Participants at the session also noted that we haven't figured out how to work together. There is so much competition among groups in some communities, as well as competition for funds. There are many agendas and causes and issues. How do we connect the agendas and issues in human services?

Sometimes we are so preoccupied with struggling for programmatic survival that we have not had enough conversations across "territories," with our peers in other programs and professions. One of the participants stated that the conflicts are not always about money. In some cases they are about principles, philosophy and strategy.

"We also need to acknowledge the tension between professionals and parents," said another member of the group. What's more, "maybe the professionals are wrong. We as professionals can learn from others." We need to find positive ways to respond to this tension.

Of course, examples of cooperation do exist in many communities. A West Coast participant said that the Los Angeles Head Start and Pre-School Program has had considerable success in developing alliances on behalf of children. The child development staff explores opportunities for cooperation with parent groups, businesses, community organizations, and others. "We base our interaction on the assumption that everyone is acting on the basis of self-interest. We explore and identify where these self-interests converge in support of children's issues.

"We avoid putting labels on people and groups," he added. *"Right wing, left wing,* and other labels don't have much meaning when we begin talking about children.

"People have built walls between each other, but almost everyone has strikingly similar goals for children, even if their approaches differ. Kids connect to everything, and they provide the avenue to deconstructing the walls between us."

"Los Angeles has over 100 cultures and 80 languages," he observed.

"You design process, curriculum, and settings that deconstruct the walls. When you do this, people can communicate, understand, and work together."

Lombardi asked the group to remember that, despite differences, we have seen some tremendous victories for kids. An extraordinary aspect of the early childhood community, however, is that "We don't celebrate our victories." Sometimes we need to take the time to acknowledge what we are accomplishing.

Today's child

In early childhood education, there is a collision between professionals and parents in regard to preparation for reading, one of the participants commented. "Early reading has become important [to parents] because of lockstep testing in every grade. Schools are saying that, if kids don't know letters and numbers, 'we're going to call them dumb.'"

Reading is just one of the areas where professionals may need to re-evaluate their strategies, or at least improve the dialogue between early childhood educators, the schools, and parents. But there are many other issues as well. "Many of today's professionals received their academic preparation 20 years ago, and children have changed." An example is parallel play. "We thought that toddlers were not ready to play on an interactive group basis until a later developmental phase. With the increasing experience of toddlers in group child care settings, however, we have discovered that they can indeed acquire the social skills necessary for group play at a very young age." We must keep learning and be open about new approaches.

Many of us have been advocates for public education. Today, however, "poor and working parents are marching to private schools and charter schools. Maybe we need to listen to them."

One participant noted that a few children view juvenile "jail" as a better "home" than their family environment. "For some, the institutional setting is their first experience with love, care, and dependable protection from risk." An inflexible strategy of reuniting families may not always be a workable solution.

We also need to discuss and explain our vision with children. We cannot assume they will understand the possibilities of democracy and community unless we explain the *how* and *why*. We say we support diversity, but how do we discuss that with kids. A negative example from the 1970s was the desegregation of a school district in Mississippi. "Without any discussion or advance notice, the school board closed the Black high school. The African American teams, history, traditions, and identities were eliminated.

Desegregation was undoubtedly to avoid a court order rather than promote diversity, but there was no communication, no explanation to the student body." An extreme example, perhaps, this case nonetheless points out that diversification without explanation can fail to be a learning experience—and indeed can be the source of increased friction and misunderstanding. We are seeing some of this expressed in resistance to immigrants, bilingualism, and affirmative action.

Another participant observed that the Mississippi episode underscores the importance of distinguishing between individual and institutional racism. "Institutional racism will not be eliminated by mixing people together or even promoting individual understanding." We cannot be one America unless we address and resolve the problem of institutional racism. "Racism cannot be stopped one person at a time." It must be rooted out at the institutional level.

One of problems that we face today is a breakdown in logic, where one of the syllogisms mistakenly goes something like: The purpose of the civil rights movement was to make everyone equal. It succeeded, and everyone is now equal. Therefore, further initiatives such as affirmative action are unnecessary.

The group discussed the issue of racism and, particularly, what to tell White children.

"Tell them that racism and injustice won't change unless they participate—become involved—in the solution," one person responded.

"We need to teach all of our children that they are both (1) individuals and (2) members of groups that have a cultural/power status." Almost no one is teaching the White children about what is happening to others.

Acknowledging reality

"Youth need caring adults, including those who have grown up in the inner city and 'made it' in affluent America. However, extending a helping hand effectively requires preparation. Adults, especially those who want to be teachers or mentors, need to understand that low-income children live in a reality that is starkly different." So began an episode recounted by presenter Geoffrey Canada.

"When I was growing up in the South Bronx, several guys came back to the ghetto to help. They talked a lot about values, and we listened politely. But they promised to organize a basketball program, and that's what really caught our interest.

"The guys went out of their way to develop a creative program that would help us develop so we could find a positive way out of ghetto problems. One of their ideas was to take us camping.

"When they said camping, we kids from the Bronx had expectations that were sharply different from theirs. We saw an exit from drab streets and apartment buildings. A chance to go to a country club! You know, hang out at a big swimming pool and maybe play some sports. A life of class. Affluence with a tall glass of lemonade, served by a waiter.

"The guys thought that camping would be a terrific bonding experience. A shared experience away from the noise and heat and broken glass.

"So we went camping, but the guys took us out to the woods. Even kids from the Bronx knew that's where bears and other wild animals lived. Would one of us get eaten or mauled?

"There we were, looking at cabins that would be condemned by a housing inspector even in the Bronx. Then there were the stinking outhouses. And trees and trees and trees where animals or other terrors could lurk.

"These guys sent us into the forest for firewood. When I was coming back to camp, I overheard the adults talking in their cabin, planning an initiation rite. They were going to take us out into the forest at night and do things.

"I ran and told my buddies that these guys are crazy. They're going to take us out and do bad things to us. These guys must be some kind of kinky freaks, I said.

"Rather than come back to camp, we kids decided to hide in the woods. The guys started to panic, thinking that they had lost their young wards. One of them decided that we might be lost. His idea was to shoot his rifle so we kids could locate the camp by following the direction of the sounds.

"When we kids heard the rifle, our reaction was hysteria. 'Run for your lives! They're going to kill us!' My friend Alan tripped on a root while running, and he fell. 'Run faster,' I shouted. 'They just shot Alan!'

"The camping foray was in total shambles, and the guys took us back to the streets of South Bronx."

"Over the years, I have thought many times about the well-intentioned efforts of these good-hearted guys. Caring alone isn't enough. Reaching out to the reality in which many of our children live requires preparation and extraordinary commitment."

Teachers and mentors must get to know their students. They can't help unless they understand the children with whom they work.

Canada's episode about the South Bronx reminded us that dialogue sessions and theory are an incomprehensible distance from the lives of many children. Charting a workable vision for 2010 will need reality checks.

Partnering with the mass media

"Children born in the coming century should expect a better life in a better world. That is going to take some planning—and some work." This was the conclusion drawn by Barbara Harrison, morning Co-Anchor for NBC4, a television station based in Washington, D.C. Following is an edited version of her presentation:

I remember when the year 2000 seemed 'forever' away. Now it is just around the corner, and it is up to all of us to make a difference in the lives of our children.

As many of you know, our slogan at NBC4 here in Washington is 'Working for You,' and the most recent addition to our mission is a new campaign we specifically call: 'Working for Children.'

We believe, as you probably do as well, that our children today face a multitude of problems—from the most serious situations of child abuse and neglect to the simple question of homework help and afterschool activities for children in our communities.

We in the news business often get caught up in chronicling the problems without helping to find the solutions.

At NBC4, we want to be sure that we not only focus on the problems, but that we also try to help ignite a fire under those who can make a difference and find ways to make some real changes to benefit all of our children.

Here are some alarming statistics. Did you know:

- The most recent survey in this country found in one year alone there were more than 3.1 million cases of child abuse reported.
- More than 1200 children died last year as a direct result of child abuse and neglect. And, since 1985, the rate of child fatalities has increased by 39 percent.
- Children are most often abused by their own families and are often trapped in homes where domestic violence is routine.
- Abused children are more likely to be involved in violent criminal activity in the future than their non-abused peers.
- If we could stop that cycle of abuse begetting abuse, think of how much money we could funnel into programs that truly benefit the children!

Let's talk about that cycle. As many of you know, I have a regular weekly segment that airs on NBC4 that we call "Wednesday's Child." These are children who have been abused, neglected, abandoned. They have ended up in the social service system as foster children awaiting permanent adoptive homes.

It is a very sad situation for most of these children because many have been in the system for years, being shuttled from one foster home to another waiting to be freed for adoption by the court. Many come into the system as babies and young toddlers, and by the time they are actually declared free to be adopted, they are older and, unfortunately, less appealing to many prospective parents who would rather have a younger child to raise as their own.

Fortunately, we've been pretty successful with this program, even though our children are considered all 'hard to place.' Many are older, many have some physical or mental delays due to poor prenatal care or drug exposure in utero. And many are part of a sibling group that we try very hard not to break up.

With all of these factors working against them, we are placing more than 40 percent of the children we present. We continue to work to make those numbers better by trying to reach more of the population—and convincing them through the children's touching stories to consider becoming adoptive parents.

Cycle of abuse and neglect

Now, let's get back to the cyclical nature of the problem. It is a known fact that many of the children who are abused, neglected and abandoned are the sons and daughters of adults who were abused, neglected, and abandoned. Statistics show that children who have been physically and sexually mistreated will perpetuate a cycle of violence against their own offspring.

It is important to add that child abuse occurs in all types of family settings and to children of all ages. Although infants and young children are more likely to receive serious or life-threatening injuries, adolescent abuse also occurs and is often unrecognized.

Sexual abuse of course is a very serious problem. Studies are showing that approximately 20 percent of the children in our country will be sexually abused in some way before they reach adulthood. That's one in five children!

Although abusers are more often male, women also may be perpetrators. Sexual abuse is most often committed by someone known to the child and frequently continues over a prolonged period of time. In fact, evidence suggests that sexual and physical abuse often occurs in successive generations of families. The cycle rarely ends unless intervention takes place.

Community partnerships

Your goal here is to look ahead, to try to prepare for the best possibilities for our children in the next century. This is an important task, and I commend you for realizing the need to make some moves now to insure a better future for our children. We must see that laying the groundwork for a better future is going to have to involve a cooperative effort by businesses, health and human service organizations, or educational institutions, and our religious communities.

We think some of the programs we have started at NBC4 are important to insuring the futures are bright for children at risk. Let me tell you a little about some of those programs that I have been involved in:

Twelve years ago, I became the spokesperson for a program we started called "Beautiful Babies Right from the Start." The goal was to try to bring down the staggeringly high rate of low birth weight and neo-natal (or infant) mortality in the nation's capital.

It happened that, coincidentally, I had just realized I was pregnant when we first thought of attacking the problem, so I offered to become the 'front person' on this campaign and ended up presenting a nine-month weekly instruction on 'How to Have a Healthy Baby.'

The news cameras followed me to every doctor's visit, and we chronicled every possible test from amino-synthesis to fetal monitoring in the last months of pregnancy. We got so many people on board we wondered if we weren't actually increasing the number of pregnancies just by making it so 'in' to be pregnant and doing it all the 'right way.'

Anyway, at the end of nine months, the program had such a following, the cameras even followed me into the delivery room, and our viewers watched me give birth right there on television.

And, as we looked at the statistics in the years that followed, we were truly gratified to see that the numbers of babies dying in the capital of the free world had actually come down significantly. Let me add that we couldn't have done it alone.

We got businesses involved, getting stores to donate gifts for prospective mothers—gifts that were redeemable only if they showed up for their prenatal visits each month.

We got hospitals to offer special after-delivery rewards, such as fancy dinners after birth for those mothers and fathers who came to birthing and child care classes.

We got Blue Cross/Blue Shield to get involved because healthy babies

> "We must see that laying the groundwork for a better future is going to have to involve a cooperative effort. . . ."
> —Barbara Harrison

can lead to healthy children with fewer health problems for 'health insurance' companies to pay for later.

We found ways to get much of the community involved, and we have had a number of television stations across the country follow our example with similar programs that they report have also been successful.

At NBC4, that program has been followed by many others. I've mentioned the Wednesday's Child project which incidentally is done in cooperation with all of the social services organizations throughout the area, in conjunction with the Washington Area Council of Local Governments. It is funded in part by the Federal Home Loan Mortgage Corporation ('Freddie Mac') simply because they saw the program and liked the fact that it was doing something for children. We have found that, as you seek community help for projects you want to do, you will find people coming out of the woodwork, just because people really do want to work to help children.

We have also started a program called 'Camp 4 Kids' which helps raise money from businesses and individuals to send children with some 'special circumstances' to camp. We have seen hundreds of children who couldn't afford such a summer experience. We also send children with cancer and AIDS to summer experiences that they have often been precluded from enjoying.

The children feel good, and we feel even better, knowing we're making even a small difference.

Operation Smile

I want to talk about the need to get involved in helping our children. Not long ago, I was called and asked if I would consider doing a story on 'Operation Smile.' It's a project that was started a few years ago in this area that takes doctors, specifically plastic surgeons, to countries around the world to perform operations to correct disfiguring facial problems on children. Because it's hard for me to turn down a story that might in some way help a child, somewhere, somehow, I said 'yes.' In some cases they wanted me to cover, the children were coming to our area for the surgery.

In fact, some of the children were local kids with disfiguring problems that had gone unattended because their parents were not financially able to afford elective medical procedures. But as you and I know, something like a cleft lip—or a large keloid growth on the side of a child's face—can affect that child's life in many profound ways.

The children that I met, both those from Third World countries, and those who were being raised right here in Washington, D.C., all suffered from a very powerful and profound lack of self esteem. The children didn't want to go to school because they didn't want to be teased by the other children.

One Vietnamese child I spoke with, through a translator, had quit school the second week of first grade because it was so painful to be chastised by the other children. He was 13 years old and because of this surgery to correct his cleft lip and pallet, he was finally going to have the opportunity to try to catch up—with the hope of one day having a normal life!

Another child I interviewed, also 13, was very bright, but in a class for children with learning disabilities simply because, throughout all of his years in school, he hung back–hoping never to be noticed, hoping no one could see the huge growth on his cheek. It was a keloid growth that formed after he scratched a chicken pox scar when he was only five years old. It had not been fixed, and something tells me that, now, he's going to catch up and be just fine!

The reward

The point of these stories is that we can't let any child fall through the cracks. We have to be vigilant enough to notice–especially those right under our noses; vigilant enough to see the difficulties children in our communities are facing.

One of the plastic surgeons I spoke with said giving new life to a child with a facial deformity was, without a doubt, the most rewarding accomplishment he as a surgeon could ever enjoy. I feel the same way about the work I do with "Wednesday's Child." I have a wonderful position as news anchor for all of our morning news shows. Yet, there is nothing that makes me feel like a real success in life than hearing that one of the children that we have featured on "Wednesday's Child" has been placed in a permanent adoptive home.

The challenge

Convincing everyone that there is truly a reward in improving the lives of children is the task we have at hand: everyone from our lawmakers here in Washington to those who make local decisions involving children's issues. From businesses to families, everyone must be involved in the effort to improve the lives of not just our own, but of all children.

Our American culture has changed so significantly over the last century that we can no longer expect that some of our old expectations will hold up. Mothers are, in greater and greater numbers, heading out to work each day along with the fathers. Extended family situations with grandparents as caregivers are rare.

We must come up with some solutions that make sense. Who will care for the children so that a mother doesn't have to worry about an inexperienced au pair being responsible for her baby. What about a child care provider working alone to take care of several babies and unwittingly putting them down to sleep with a blanket that ends up suffocating them both?

The stories of childcare gone awry come across my desk almost every day. As a working mother, I know the challenges of trying to come up with realistic solutions for the care of our children.

And for the children growing up in poverty, what about them? In this wonderful country, where we can send back pictures of the rocks on Mars and analyze their make-up, we still have children who wake up with empty bellies and go to bed hungry, too.

And yet, we're working hard to end welfare. This is perhaps a good idea, but how will we really fix the problems that make welfare a necessity for so many?

If so many children are still recognized as 'poor,' who is going to make up the difference in providing the services these children and their families will need? It has to be us!

We cannot turn our backs. If families can't afford the high cost of expensive day care with both parents—or single parents—having to work, who is going to make sure we have good, affordable care for the children? Who is going to make sure kids don't have to unlatch a lock and stay home alone waiting for working parents to return at night?

Who is going to be the advocates for those children?

It has to be us!

Preparing children (and society) for one America

Geoffrey Canada told the group that Americans know better. Deep down, most of us understand what children need. The problem is that we cast logic and commitment aside when we cross the boundaries from affluent neighborhoods to those in the inner city.

"If you make enough money, you live in a different America. The longer you live in the Affluent America, the more likely you are to blame the people of the Other America—rather than the underlying conditions—for their problems."

Canada focused on the public schools to illustrate the problems inherent in building a 21st century democracy and to challenge the participants of the **Children of 2010** to find solutions. He spoke on August 5th, the final day of the dialogue series. Mr. Canada, who is president of the Rheedlen Centers for Children and Families in New York City, is the author of *Reaching Up for Manhood and Fist Stick Knife Gun: A Personal History of Violence in America.*

We ought to know

"I get tired of explaining what poor kids need." Whenever low-income neighborhoods in New York ask for more extracurricular activities, there are stringent guidelines—usually tied to raising the reading levels of students. Otherwise, there is virtually no public support for needed activities and opportunities.

Canada contrasted two school settings: In middle-income neighborhoods, students can select a host of activities such as sports, drama, band, orchestra, computer club, and more. These do not have to be justified on the basis of raising test scores. Everyone simply knows that these are nurturing and broadening resources for youth development. Yet, in low-income schools, most of these activities are absent.

He challenged the group: "Line up 20 parents, describe two public schools, and ask them which they want their children to attend. Without any other details, just describe the extracurricular and enrichment activities of the two settings that I have contrasted. All 20 parents will select the school with the extra opportunities. It doesn't matter where they live, whether these are middle-income or low-income parents; they all know which educational setting makes sense. They all want these supports"

Check the logic

"In the wake of the Jonesboro incident in which two children killed four girls and a teacher, media representatives called me. They wanted an explanation. How could these things happen to our youth?

"I didn't want to talk with the media about youth violence. How do I tell them this is old news? Thousands of kids die because of violence." Affluent America is shocked with the idea that violence, common to inner city youth, can occur elsewhere, even in the rural and seemingly pastoral communities of Arkansas.

There is a failure of logic; a false perception of cause and effect. According to this aberrant logic, inner city youth suffer from violence because they are: inner city, people of color, ghetto, different. Race and poverty become an explanation of the violence.

The fact is that some kids are not getting what they need to develop as healthy humans. Youth violence can happen in the suburbs and countryside, in nice neighborhoods, in small town schools. *Youth violence is happening in nice communities.*

Usually, soul-searching about the causes of violence occurs only when race cannot be used as an explanation. Then, the real problems that youth encounter must be identified.

It's time we begin acknowledging the problems that youth encounter, including those who live in low-income neighborhoods. Race must no longer be used as an excuse, an "easy out" for avoiding a commitment to solve the underlying problems.

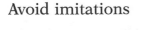

Avoid imitations

Canada recounted the school experiences of his sister's two children in South Carolina. One attends public school; the other private school. The child who attends public school averages 35 minutes of homework each night, but the one in private school almost always has at least 4 hours of preparation.

Are public schools merely delivering an imitation of an education? Going through the motions? In a society where jobs are demanding increased abilities to absorb and apply knowledge, we are shortchanging public school children if we fail to support them with full academic competency.

In the inner city, this may be another example of our society's flawed logic: We demand that middle-income kids attain academic competency, but we lower our expectations for the ghetto. We use excuses like *socioeconomic problems*, *disadvantaged*, *poor*, *special education*, and *English-limited pupils*.

Somewhere we have lost sight of the fact that low-income children need exactly the same things as other kids: A real education. Preparation for postsecondary education. Competency to hold a job. Ability to function as an informed and active citizen in a democracy.

"A while ago, there was a reunion of the alumni of the Rheedlen Centers. We old guys were having a great time on a sports field, playing games and pretending to be super jocks. A kid from the neighborhood approached us, selling T-shirts. Several of us bought them, and an alumnus gave him a $20 and asked for change. The kid was clueless about the simple subtraction required to make the change."

"What kind of society leaves some of its children academically naked, unprotected by the skills needed for basic survival?"

Demand performance

Leaders are held accountable for performance in almost every corporation and agency in America. A CEO who fails to turn around a company or increase profits will likely be shown the door by shareholders. A mayor who fails to satisfy most of the voters will likely be thrown out.

Public schools are a notable exception. Students can fail to learn, but the principal remains on the job for 20 years. Teachers who are incompetent receive the same percentage raises as those who get the job done.

Educators, policymakers, and society in general rationalize the failure of the public schools to educate in low-income communities. The pupils have problems. The students aren't interested in learning. The children have disabilities or limited aptitudes. The parent's aren't supportive.

But these rationalizations are bunk. "I have seen different school districts within New York City—working with the same per pupil expenditures, the same curriculum, and the same populations of children—where the educational outcomes are markedly different. Most of the students in one district will be succeeding; most in the neighboring district will be failing."

"How do you explain this in any way other than leadership? Principals and school administrators are responsible for selecting teachers, guiding them, evaluating them, retaining them, or firing them.

"In other industries, leaders, managers, and professionals worry about raises (or even losing their jobs) if they don't achieve results. They work extra hours—evenings and weekends if necessary to boost their performance. They urgently search for solutions until they find them.

"In the public schools, the work culture is out of step with the rest of America. They quit at 3 o'clock, even if the children are falling behind academically. They enjoy their weekends and vacations, even if they are delivering an imitation of education, rather than the real thing.

"Twenty years ago, we placed the responsibility on the doorstep of White administrators, principals, and teachers. Today, educators of color are often the ones falling down on the job. Either way, our children are being cheated unless they get a good education.

"Firing nonperformers gets results. It sends a message to the other educators: You must make sure that the kids receive a real education, or you will lose your job. You're responsible.

"Perhaps teachers who are not getting results need to stay at school until 4, 5, or 6 o'clock. Maybe they need to come in weekends. Maybe the perks of shorter hours and pay raises should be reserved for the educators who are getting the expected results. After all, these are the things that happen in other industries when employees fail to measure up to performance standards.

"All children can learn, but not all teachers can teach all children to learn. Our teachers in the inner city must be those who can perform. Anything less will be only an imitation of education.

"People of color must have equal access to a *good* education."

Students in low-income communities need public schools that are accountable for academic performance. Demanding anything less would lock millions of children into a dead-end, hope-dead future.

Explore the union issue

Fostering public schools that work will require addressing issues related to teachers unions, Canada said. Otherwise, accountability for educator performance may be blunted by provisions of contracts that protect seniority and often require lock-step raises for all teachers regardless of ability. In some cases, principals may even be regarded as "labor" rather than "management," thereby severing accountability for decisionmaking and leadership.

This is a difficult issue for some individuals who like to consider themselves as pro-labor. Yet, doesn't a consumer who buys a union-shop automobile expect a product that is safe and dependable? A factory employee who performs defective workmanship that endangers the public would not be tolerated in the 1990s. We should expect no less accountability for the educational safety of our children.

Regardless of what dialogue participants think, however, parents are already making their decisions. "People don't want reform anymore," Canada declared. "The school system is broke, and the parents want out."

Given the deep-seated concerns of parents, perhaps the time has come to renegotiate expectations. Educators in public schools have a great deal to lose unless they respond quickly and dramatically.

Rethink public education

It is urgent that we rethink public education. Some of the old strategies may no longer work, nor may former assumptions be valid. For example, must successful completion of algebra continue to be the "litmus test" of ability to pursue a college education, when few of us adults actually use equations in our everyday lives? Is placing huge numbers of males of color in special education simply an excuse, an indication of our failure to teach?

We also need to look at how tests are used. While they can be used to diagnose needs or monitor progress, tests are used too often as a means for sorting children into groups of winners and losers. Tests are used to track students, even in elementary school. Before they turn age 10, some kids are "sent to the back of the bus" for the remainder of their lifelong journey, based on these tests.

Many children in the inner city do not have a clue about how to take tests, Canada added. On a timed test, they don't know they should skip over a difficult problem rather than wasting 15 minutes on it. They don't understand that it is a game like basketball, and you can improve your score simply by understanding the rules.

If you believe that all children can learn, that should affect our approaches to education. The challenge is not to fit the child to the educational system, but to fit the learning environment to the child.

In rethinking education, we must also address the implications of the technological revolution. The Internet and other interactive media provide the means by which the next generation will access and organize information. It can literally put the world of knowledge at each person's fingertips. Access to information technology will change the playing field for jobs, learning, and lifestyle. We must learn how to level the playing field so that our children in low-income communities have access to the future.

Welcome the parents

Canada emphasized the parent-child relationship. "I have seen what determined parents can accomplish under difficult circumstances. I have seen them challenge 'special education' labels, resulting in 'mainstream' academic success for their children."

"I don't know how she did it, but my mother made sure that we did our school work. With today's easy access to the diversions of music and television, parental guidance is especially important." Homes need to develop a "culture of learning."

Parents have quite a few challenges in keeping up with the schools. Innovative programs that reinvent teaching programs every few years can throw parents for a loop. Thinks like "new math" can make it very difficult for parents to support their children's school efforts.

Parents in poor communities do not have the time or resources to challenge school systems on their own. Yet, there exists the potential for change. After all, they share most of the same concerns as middle-income parents and prospective corporate employers.

Hang in there with young people

"I am convinced that we give up far too early on young people," Canada added. "We have a belief system in this country that, if you mess up early in life, you can't recover. This simply is not true.

"I have seen young adults get serious about their lives. After criminal justice encounters. After school failures. After forays into drugs. But in their teens or early twenties, they sometimes wake up and get a new start in life. "Those who struggle for a new start may finish high school or enroll in community college. They work at putting their lives together, and we as a society need to be there to support them."

Are we giving up on public schools without a fight?

Parents are desperate to gain access to a decent education for their children, Canada said. In New York City, 50,000 low- and moderate-income families applied for 10,000 vouchers so that they could send their children to private and parochial schools, where they hoped children would have better access to a real education. People of color, after all, have the same hopes and ambitions for their children as do other Americans.

Canada noted that parents are expressing a great deal of interest in alternatives to public schools, such as public vouchers and charter schools.

Parents may endorse the ideal of "public schools" and democracy in education, but they do not want to sacrifice their own children as fodder for experiments in educational reform.

"I hope that my 9-month-old son will be able to attend public school and receive a good education," Canada said. "I believe that our society will lose a great deal if we abandon our public schools. I suspect that, in the long run, the alternatives will not produce equal access to quality education for all of our children."

Many of the underlying problems would need to be addressed if public schools were to make a comeback. In addition to the performance issues, there are problems related to deteriorating tax bases in central cities, decreasing per pupil expenditures in some districts (when adjustments are made for inflation), and the decreasing commitment of voters to support the schools.

Could the stampede to alternatives create a "separate and unequal" educational environment reminiscent of segregated schools? Certainly many civil rights advocates make this point and rally behind teachers unions, regardless of how dismal the performance of the public schools.

There are few easy answers for parents with flesh-and-blood children who cannot wait for future reform.

For democracy's sake, we must educate well

"In the aftermath of the Los Angeles civil unrest," Canada told the group, "I was invited to a meeting in Harlem because people were concerned that rioting might occur there also. I didn't see much hope expressed by the community residents who were at the meeting.

"They felt abandoned. They said that the people in shirts and ties weren't willing to do anything about the problem. I looked around and noticed that I was the only guy with a tie."

Our society has shown an alarming lack of commitment to public education in recent years. Per pupil spending has not kept up with inflation and economic growth, and taxpayers in some parts of the country are resisting budget increases for schools.

If we intend to have a democracy in this country, we must educate well. If we are committed to *one* America for all people, Canada concluded, we must give every child equal access to a real education.

Moving forward

Origins of the dialogue. The dialogue planner who developed the concept for the **Children of 2010** session said that the program had its origins in 1996 when she immersed herself in the culture of the Dominican Republic. To look at her own culture, and the future, she sought to step apart, experience another culture, and learn its Spanish language.

From that vantage point, she wrote a paper on the children of 2010, and it became the baseline for the program. The strategy was modified through her conversations with the National Association for the Education of Young Children, and it continued to evolve throughout the program.

Dialogue, after all, is a process of intentional evolution, and the three dialogue sessions have broadened her own perspective, as it did for most other participants. "In a sense, we are redesigning our view of democracy and ethnicity. Just as previous generations of Americans have struggled with reinventing their vision of democracy, we are continuing to do so here."

Change and the changeless. "Change is one of the constants that we have identified, and it underlies the necessity of redefining democracy in each generation," she said. We must distinguish between changeless principles—based on enduring values—and the strategies by which we seek to advance them.

"It is easy to become so enamored of our strategies that we are unwilling to shed them, even when they no longer work well. A benefit of the dialogue process is that we can reflect upon and challenge our strategies, seeking new tools that are better suited to furthering our unchanging commitment to a humane society, an inclusive democracy."

Possibilities of school reform. Educational reform—one of the most pressing needs of the children of 2010—may be possible because of the forces at work that support change, hoped one of the dialogue participants. "It may not take the collapse of the large systems. Parent dissatisfaction and the trends toward enrollment in private and charter schools may provide an opportunity to negotiate a new compact with the school systems."

A long-range vision. One of the meeting planners encouraged participants to gauge progress over the long term. "So often we feel like we have failed, when that is really not the case. Too often we measure our progress from the vantage point of too brief a timeframe. One of the themes of the **Children of 2010** program is adjusting our perspective to the long-range view. Our vision will require sustained action, and many of the advances we seek can only be measured over years and decades.

"This is not intended as an excuse for accepting the status quo. Rather it is a challenge. The well-being of children and youth requires our lifelong commitment; not simply involvement in a program or campaign."

The gift of yourself. "In building on a vision of democracy and diversity, it is important to represent yourself in your work," added a participant. "This is important to me as an African American woman. Putting ourselves, our individuality, into our commitment to a better future is how we make certain that democracy will be truly inclusive."

Think nationally, act locally. Too often, our work to improve the lives of children has been at the national level, without sufficient follow-through within states and communities. National meetings, advocacy, policy initiatives, and demonstration programs are only the starting point. To make a difference in the lives of many more children, we must greatly increase action and change at the local level.

Change requires working with the people in our own community. This will require breaking down the walls between different professions and institutions. It calls on us to listen to parents and families, including those who are quite different from us. More than likely, it will mean that we must set aside our favorite assumptions and strategies, as well as worn-out labels such as "liberal" and "conservative."

Most of our neighbors are interested in the wellbeing of children, though they will express this interest with different priorities, rhetoric, strategies, and languages

Reflecting

Violent Streets of Childhood[36]

From *fist stick knife gun* by Geoffrey Canada

The summer is the worst time for children I know. More of them are outside. Too hot and too boring to be inside. There are few jobs for the teenagers. Life is lived and lost on the streets. By the time they shot little Luis in the head in August, sixty other innocent bystanders under sixteen had been shot that year in New York City. There would be more. It really is getting worse. Too many guns, too much crack, too few jobs, so little hope.

America has had a love affair with violence and guns. It's our history, we teach it to all of our young. The Revolution, the "taming of the West," the Civil War, the world wars, and on and on. Guns, justice, righteousness, freedom, liberty–all tied to violence.

Nation Still Struggling to Make the Grade on Violence

AMA National Report Card shows slight improvements, but overall incidence rate still unacceptable

(Chicago—June 11, 1996) The American Medical Association handed the nation a "D" today in its annual Report Card on Violence. Despite increased public awareness and commitment to change, AMA President Lonnie Bristow, M.D., noted that "the country is still struggling to control its number one public health crisis."

"It is disheartening to see an overall "D" again this year," said Dr. Bristow.

The American Medical Association's "National Report Card on Violence," documents the status of family violence; sexual assault; public violence and virtual violence (violence in entertainment) in America. Grades are assigned by an AMA panel based on the latest available information, statistics and research.

"The real question is, 'Are we safer today than we were a year ago?' The answer is no," said Dr. Bristow. "This country will not pass the test until we can safely walk our streets at night and send our children to school alone without fear."

This year's Report Card rewards an increase in public awareness and new federal and local initiatives aimed at ending family violence and entertainment violence, with a slight grade increase of C and D+ respectively. But, an F in public violence and D- in sexual assault keep the overall average grade firmly at a "D."

"Kids tell us that it's easy to buy a gun, but it's cheaper to rent one by the hour," said Dr. Bristow. "When it is easier to get a gun in this country than it is to get a library card, we know we are heading in the wrong direction."

The grades: nation receives overall "D"

Again this year, the nation received an overall "D" which reflects the average of grades assigned to the following four categories:

"C" Family violence (spousal/partner abuse, elder abuse, child physical/sexual abuse, and suicide) This grade is up from a C- last year because of a dramatic increase in public awareness and education—particularly on domestic violence. Credit was also given for initiatives such as the 1994 Crime Bill, which is encouraging and funding anti-domestic violence programs. Corporations are becoming more aware of the issues, and some communities have begun to develop prevention and intervention models.

The AMA and the American Bar Association (ABA) have published a comprehensive "Community Guide"of model grass-roots anti-violence programs and are conducting a series of regional meetings to teach multi-disciplinary teams from each state strategies for building coordinated community responses to violence in their communities. Also, in 1995 the AMA Alliance launched "Stop America's Violence Everywhere" (SAVE), which involved physicians' spouses across the country simultaneously conducting more than 650 anti-violence initiatives to help victims reclaim their lives. But, most programs like these take years to bear fruit. In the meantime, incidence rates of domestic violence, child abuse, elder abuse, and suicide remain high, and research continues to document staggering direct and indirect costs.

"D-" Sexual assault (sexual assault, stranger rape and date/acquaintance/spousal rape) The grade remains unchanged, reflecting no improvement from last year. This crime remains dramatically under-reported, largely due to negative societal attitudes and myths about rape that leave victims with feelings of shame and embarrassment. According to a 1995 survey of 1,965 eighth and ninth graders: 11 percent agreed that if a girl says "no" to sex she usually means "yes;" half said that being raped was sometimes the victim's fault; and, 40 percent agreed that girls who wear sexy clothes are "asking to be raped." Victims also avoid reporting because they fear court procedures that too often scrutinize and judge their behavior rather than their offender's. An estimated two-thirds of attacks go unreported, making apprehension and conviction of offenders nearly impossible. After declaring sexual assault a "silent violent epidemic" in November of 1995, the AMA began a public awareness campaign to encourage victims to talk to their doctors. The AMA also distributed guidelines to help physicians better identify, treat and refer victims of sexual assault. Still, much more needs to be done to address this problem. Sexual assault is not a societal priority though it is said to be our nation's most expensive crime.

"F" Public violence (juvenile/gang violence, gun violence, civil violence and drug violence) This grade constitutes no change from last year because public violence continues to elude our control. Violence rates in certain areas (homicide for example) did show stabilization and, in some cases, decline. For example, homicide rates in New York City dropped 25 percent from 1994 to 1995. However, these rates do not necessarily foretell a trend. In 1995, homicide rates in Minneapolis rose 56 percent. And compared to 1965, the national murder rate per capita is almost double (1965: 5.1 per 100,000; 1994: 9.0). Most troubling are the rising rates of juvenile violence and crime which may indicate rising rates of violence in the coming year. And while there are some positive public policy accomplishments that offer hope, such as the recently enacted federal anti-terrorism law, overall trends in juvenile, gun, civil and drug violence continue to rise. The enormous weight of violent crime in every segment of American life has increasingly led to mounting fears and individuals "re-arming" in order to protect themselves and their families by violent means. Increasing poverty, illiteracy, drug and alcohol addiction, racial unrest, disrespect for authority and the dissolution of the American family continue to fuel a society of fear, vigilantism, paranoia, and retribution.

"D+" "Virtual Violence"—Violence in entertainment (television violence, music violence, film violence, video violence, computer and Cyberspace violence) "Virtual violence" refers to violence that is not physically experienced, but which carries a lasting psychosocial effect on the individual. This grade is up from a D last year as a result of an enormous increase in public awareness, passage of the Communications Law and a commitment to a new voluntary rating system. However, there is no evidence that virtual violence is on the decline—yet. Violent programming is still rampant in all forms of entertainment and consumers are still buying it. While the explosion of computer technology has created exciting new entertainment mediums, it also presents new avenues of concern. Although there has been promising movement in the right direction, actual progress will be judged by how aggressively and successfully interventions are implemented by government and industry and utilized by the public. The AMA encourages American parents' to get involved and use these tools diligently to reduce the level of virtual violence they and their families are exposed to.

Solutions: a challenge to America

"If we hope to redeem the lives of our young people and stem the tide of violence, each of us must become a peacemaker in the midst of a battleground," said Dr. Bristow.

Concerns about violence are high on most people's agenda and fears about one's personal safety are all too common, but signs of hope are apparent as well. Events of the past year suggest as a nation we have chosen not to simply wring our hands about violence but that we are willing to undertake efforts to lessen its incidence and prevalence. But change will demand our continued commitment.

"Every community should have a comprehensive integrated intervention plan to bring all our strengths to bear on this problem," said Dr. Bristow. America's challenge for the coming year is not only to see that federal initiatives fulfill their potential, but also to assure that we continue to build channels of communication and cooperation between disciplines, allowing communities to work together to get the job done. Health care workers, teachers, law enforcement, social services, religious leaders, the media—every person has something to give that can make a difference.

"Like any disease, violence must be stopped at the source," said Dr. Bristow." Solutions will come from each of us working together to stop the violence and begin a cure."

Eskimos Warm to the Digital Age
by Doug Fine
Copyright © 1998. *The Washington Post*
Sunday, August 9, 1998; Page C01

I had never seen a Web site materialize so fast. I was in Toksook Bay, a largely subsistence Yup'ik Eskimo village in western Alaska, 400 miles from Russia and 5,700 miles from Washington. My host, Greg Lincoln, a thirtyish Yup'ik man, was demonstrating the cutting edge of wireless digital technology.

I was greeted by an immediate sound blast of Yup'ik voices accompanied by an animated image of Lincoln's daughter stomping in traditional clothing. Lincoln's Web site (members.aol.com/glincoln45/ frame.html) celebrates traditional Eskimo life by displaying dancing rituals and stereophonic singing. I clicked on an icon, and was offered crafts made by his family and friends for sale in a "Village Mall." Chalk up one cluster of indigenous people who don't need to leave traditional lands in order to make a cash living.

The key to Lincoln's demonstration was a small box on the windowsill of his house which pulls down satellite-beamed transmissions powerful enough to provide him with Internet access at bandwidths something like three times faster than the current standard at American corporations and 10 times faster than in most American homes—all without a telephone line. What's more, Lincoln can keep his Internet connection all day—at no cost.

A fledgling company called Alaska Wireless is installing the boxes in Toksook Bay in the hope of showing that the hundreds of millions of scattered people worldwide who were left out of the Telephone Age will be able to leapfrog directly and cheaply into the Digital Age.

My visit to Toksook Bay—a village of 700 people which got its first telephone in 1980—brought home to me some fundamental issues of the digital age: Will the ability to communicate freely in the impending Era Without Wires come to be accepted as a fundamental right? Will digital communication networks become public property, with every citizen having access? Or will the exchange of digital information be routed and controlled by private firms who charge for the service? In a world of potentially nearly infinite bandwidth, will the spirit of the market prevail—or the spirit of the First Amendment? Is the specter of government involvement more of a threat than a savior? Those are the questions that are being worked out here on the tundra.

The total cost for the Alaska Wireless system in Toksook Bay was about $10,000—to connect the whole town. Under the old system with the telephone company, it cost about $4,300 to have an Internet pipe installed in one house, not to mention the astronomical per-minute bills for being online. And the traditional phone lines inevitably create the delays inherent in waiting for a graphics-heavy Web page to download via America Online with a 28.8 modem. That is a state of affairs I wouldn't wish on anybody.

A slight problem is the region's telephone company monopoly, the Eskimo-owned United Utilities. Its managers accurately see the Alaska Wireless system as competition with its expensive bush telephone network. They insist, wireless advocates say, that Alaska Wireless is subject to certain conditions of the federal grants that are used to pay for part of their Toksook Bay connection. Some of these are provisions of the 1996 Telecommunications Act that arguably require that the technology only be installed in educational institutions or government buildings, not in private residences. The telephone company says that some of the complications are arising because of provisions that not even everyone in the industry fully understands.

"We're the local carrier there," Steve Hamlen, president of United Utilities, explains. "We are required to provide service to everyone, and we owe $22 million in subsidized loans we took to provide that. We're concerned about losing customers and revenue to a wireless provider because we're required to retain an infrastructure to serve everyone."

Hamlen acknowledges that this is a "very complex" time in telecommunications, and that by the time professionals get a grasp on nuances and potential conflicts inherent in new laws, "the rules and the technology will have changed." This is exactly why access to the digital spectrum should remain as open as possible.

As for providing Internet service to rural communities like Toksook Bay, Hamlen says, "We're capable of providing high speed connections to the Internet with the existing copper system."

Many people in the region have a hard time sympathizing with a company that cites nuances in federal law in order to preserve its monopoly, especially when Alaska Wireless isn't making big bucks on the installation in Toksook Bay. It's irrational to accept the argument that the actual inhabitants of the village should be denied blazing Internet connections because the technology available to them is too good. It was a telling oversight that when William Kennard, the chair of the Federal Communications Commission, paid a visit to Alaska in June, he didn't even mention the wireless technology. To his credit, he did open discussion about allowing competition in rural telephone service.

But the details of telecommunications policy, while important, are increasingly beside the point. While the lawyers posture and the regulators reconsider, the digital revolution is taking hold in Toksook Bay.

Greg Lincoln's home looks like another of the functional, wooden houses that replaced traditional Eskimo sod homes after the Bureau of Indian Affairs moved into Toksook Bay in the 1950s. But the gear inside was an immediate giveaway that there is something unconventional going on in the house. I mistook Lincoln's 200 megahertz Wintel Machine for "a 386," revealing my non-techie stripes. As a Cossack (pronounced locally as "GUSS-sack," a generic term for white-looking guy), it was assumed I should know all about this kind of technology.

People often instinctively associate the advent of the Digital Age and all of its tools with the automatic decline of cultural heterogeneity and general attention span. Yup'ik elder Philip Moses told me that he recognizes that the skills he uses to build kayaks, seal-gut parkas and fox-hair boots have been disappearing village-wide, along with the place names his generation uses to identify every hill, river and valley within 50 miles. But, with his daughter interpreting, Moses also said that Yup'ik cultural awareness is higher now than it has been for a few decades, "and some of the new technology can be used to teach new generations about their culture and the outside world." In Toksook Bay, that is an endorsement from a high place.

Lincoln foresees wide-ranging applications of high bandwidth Internet connectivity in Yup'ik life. He envisions an Internet-based radio news program that would spread regional and world headlines to isolated communities in the Yukon-Kuskakwim Delta—in the Yup'ik language. (The only previous Yup'ik radio program was canceled a few years ago for budget reasons.) There may be bureaucratic objections to wireless connectivity in Toksook Bay, but the technology is available to fulfill Lincoln's ambitions at a low cost. Internet transmissions via the wireless system will be free to produce and transmit, as long as you've got a recorder and some Real Audio software.

The promise of digital technology is most evident in Toksook Bay's Nelson Island School. Kids whose first language is Yup'ik have been studying Spanish in front of video-conferencing monitors showing lectures being given in North Dakota. A 6-year-old sweetheart named Alicia told me about her e-mail pen pals around the world. Piano lessons are given on virtual online keyboards while, outside, fisherman return from the herring hunt. Children in Toksook Bay will now have choices: medical school or subsistence hunting or French cooking or Mayan archeology. Or maybe all of the above.

Eskimos traditionally have had an incredibly pragmatic attitude about incorporating outside technology, according to teacher Jim Mitchell, a 12-year resident of Toksook Bay who was responsible for arranging much of the village's wireless technology.

The rifle has proved useful, he pointed out, and the Global Positioning System, a locator device useful for traveling in areas without maps, has been widely adopted. "If the Internet adds something to their culture, they'll use it," Mitchell says. "Otherwise, they'll abandon it."

Toksook Bay illustrates that the world's move to digital existence will likely be shaped by both market forces and the unquenchable human desire to communicate. International lines are already being blurred by the decentralization inherent in the Internet, and it is hard to justify the selling off of bandwidth to the highest bidder when it's arguable whether such bandwidth can even be owned. Don't worry, market forces can be loosed and huge companies can make their profit launching satellites and creating private digital networks for other huge companies that want to use them. But when little boxes on windowsills can put Bangladesh in touch with Botswana, the old rules of the game no longer apply.

What struck me most about the matter-of-fact way the Yup'ik community is using digital technology is how practically it is applied when it is truly needed. It is the first media technology I have seen that neither waters down a local culture nor attempts to sell products to it. Rather, the wireless digital technology helps to preserve local traditions and creates a symbiosis with the wider world that seems to have less and less time or use for non-market cultures.

Doug Fine, who has reported for *The Washington Post* from Burma, Laos, and Rwanda, is directing a feature film in Alaska called *Migration.*

Dialoging about a vision for children

1. As you near the conclusion of this book, write a list of facts, ideas, and insights that you have discovered.

2. If you are in regular contact with parents, ask them what improvements they would like to see for the children of 2010.

3. What role do you see parents playing in creating a good future for their children?

4. Review the South Bronx episode under the "Acknowledging Reality" heading. Can you think of instances where well-intended people and programs have failed to be effective in connecting with young people and their needs?

5. Review the AMA "report card" on violence. Do you agree with the rating of "F" for public violence? What are the implications for the children of 2010? What can we do to make 2010 a safer place for children?

6. Review the article describing how an Eskimo village is using technology to improve communication and preserve culture. Can technology empower other communities, groups, families, and children?

7. How would you like to see the mass media improve opportunities for children?

8. What is your own assessment of the public schools? What solutions do you propose?

9. Why isn't there better continuity between early childhood education, K to 12 schools, and postsecondary education?

10. Do you agree with Canada's assertion that society gives up on young people far too soon?

11. Are you now ready to outline your own vision statement about the children of 2010?

12. If you are coming to grips with a vision, what are you going to do about it?

13. Are you planning any action or changes for the children of 2010?

Letter to the Children of 2010

Focusing

We attempted to capture the group's overall reflections and vision by writing a "time capsule" letter to the children of 2010. We are sharing our letter with you:

August 1998

Beloved Children of 2010:

When you open the time capsule and read this letter, you may be surprised to discover that dozens of people have devoted many hours in 1998 to thinking about you. Over the next 11½ years, we seek to create a future that affirms, protects, respects, and develops your considerable potential as 21st century Americans. Ultimately, you yourselves will be the judge of the extent to which our vision was accurate or our hopes for you have been realized.

This letter is from the people who attended a series of meetings appropriately named **"Children of 2010."** We have taken the time to participate in these discussions because your generation will face unprecedented challenges. In part, this is because the United States is in the midst of so much change: demography, economy, institutional practices, public policy, technology, and much more. In part, however, it is also a matter of addressing the historic problem of making democracy work in a nation where over 98 percent of the population is derived from many other lands.

The challenges and risks that you face, however, are accompanied by unprecedented opportunity. Historically, we Americans have expressed an uncommon idea—welcoming the peoples of the world and building a land of opportunity based on hard work and the strengths of many cultures. In practice, we have fallen short of our vision. Yet, in your generation, we have reason to hope that the American dream will continue to evolve into reality for all.

We are writing this letter just before our last meeting. It will help us review all of the topics we have discussed so we can gain a better perspective on what our priorities should be for shaping a positive future for your generation. We are sharing our reflections with you because we want each of you to know that we love you, care about your future, and hope you will find a new century of opportunity.

Hope

Our group surveyed the American past and present, acknowledging that the ideals of our nation have gone unfulfilled on many occasions. Injustice, lack of access to opportunity, and even basic obstacles to health and safety have detracted from the American dream. Notwithstanding, we believe that their is hope—both for us and for you.

Things can and do change for the better. Universal access to education for children is an idea that was not broadly implemented throughout the United States until the late 19th century. Child labor laws to protect young people from unhealthy and brutal industrial conditions were not enacted by Congress until the early 20th century. Equal access to public education was not decided by the Supreme Court until the middle of the 20th century. People of color could not access most hotels and restaurants in the south until the past 30 to 35 years. Requiring employers to give women equal pay for equal work is a startlingly recent event. Public acknowledgment of the right of children with disabilities to obtain an education is also quite recent. These are but a few examples of the changes that have occurred.

Each of these changes—gradually transforming the rhetoric of the American dream into reality—has come at a price. Each change required leadership, years of persistence, controversy and opposition, and sometimes peril. In the face of injustice and the slowness of change, it can be tempting to resort to hopelessness and despair, but remember that even in the darkest night there is hope. As Martin Luther King said 35 years before our letter to you, "Let us not wallow in the valley of despair. I say to you, my friends, we have the difficulties of today and tomorrow. I still have a dream. It is a dream deeply rooted in the American dream."

There is hope. Use it for survival, change, and prosperity.

Demographics

At our meetings, we learned of major population changes that are already underway, which you will see more clearly in 2010. The Hispanic population is expected to rise dramatically, particularly in the southwest and west, where Latinos will constitute a majority of the population in some states. The African American population will increase—representing a majority of the population in certain southern states. Asian Americans will also constitute a larger share of the overall U.S. population.

In addition to higher fertility rates for many people of color—compared to non-Hispanic Whites, immigration will also play a major role in population growth, with a large portion of the influx expected to be from Asia and Latin America.

You will also live with the largest population of older Americans in U.S. history. Compared to your generation, a larger proportion of them will be non-Hispanic Whites. More of them will also live much longer lives than our parents did. Please try to keep a line of communication open to these older folks because (smile) in 2010 you will categorize most of us meeting participants in that age range. Many of us care about young people and the American dream, and we can often be your allies.

Working together

During the first two centuries following the American Revolution, non-Hispanic Europeans dominated U.S. culture, politics, and industry. You will be seeing that change, at least gradually. You young people will be at the vanguard of that change, but during the last half of the 21st century—within your lifetime, demographers forecast that people of color will constitute the *majority* of U.S. citizens (and voters and workers and parents and consumers).

What will be unique in the history of the United States is that, during your adult life, no racial or ethnic group will have a clearcut majority. At the state level, diverse voters may sometimes have to form alliances in order to seek an electoral majority. At the national level, the states will be extraordinarily diverse: Northern heartland states will likely have non-Hispanic European majorities, the northeast and northwest will probably be heterogeneous, and we have already noted that African Americans or Hispanics will constitute a majority in a number of southern and southwestern states—as well as California. Federal lawmaking and governance will require cooperation among Americans with many different cultural backgrounds.

But many employers are already telling us that, when you are ready for a job, you will be *working* together to earn a living. Businesses and agencies need employees who can contribute to work teams that will often include individuals from diverse backgrounds. Your customers, both locally and worldwide, will also reflect many different cultures.

One of your greatest challenges, then, will be to gain experience in teaming and succeeding with people from many different backgrounds. By doing so, you will be fulfilling a longstanding dream of e pluribus unum—out of many peoples, one nation.

Respect

Working together requires respect, and participants at our 1998 meetings discussed the importance of respect for each person's individuality. We probed the ways in which it is denied to many children and their families. Some of these conversations were quite vivid, reflecting personal experiences of rejection by teachers, institutions, and neighbors. Many of the bad experiences were fueled by racism and other prejudice.

Our notion of *respect* is more than simply being polite. It acknowledges and values individuality. Respect searches for appropriate, individualized responses to each person's uniqueness. This has been a difficult lesson for our institutions such as schools to learn because we inherited the mindset of the industrial age—where mass production, standardization, branding, and uniformity were goals. In 1998, we are still grappling with how to establish a learning environment that develops unique potential and talent, rather than stamping out Model Ts while neglecting children who don't fit the mold. It is our fondest wish that we will have solved this problem by the time you read our letter.

We hope to make both ourselves and our institutions more respectful of and responsive to individual differences. This must address the problem of unequal access to opportunity, for each one of you has a right to reach for the American dream. Further, we believe that creating *fair access to opportunity* will benefit every child in America. There are so many physical differences, learning styles, interests, and abilities among all children! Each of you deserves the respect of an individualized response that gives you access to your wonderful potential.

Equipment for achievement

One of our younger participants reminded us that the pursuit of opportunity is like a race. Learning, educational achievement, personal development, and career opportunities all require stamina, persistence, and *equipment*. On this latter point is where quite a few children in the past (and in 1998) have failed to gain fair access to opportunity. Using this analogy, some children have struggled to run the race barefooted, while others have had access to quality sneakers and even roller skates and bicycles.

In 1998, we are struggling with how to make sure that every child has access to the basic equipment needed to pursue the American dream. We cannot guarantee that you will win first place, and you indeed have a responsibility for preparing and doing your best; but a passion of ours is to make certain that each of you in 2010 will have the equipment to pursue and finish the race with a sense of dignity and fulfillment.

Most of the "equipment" that you need is fairly obvious: an affirming and nurturing environment, access to education and learning, health care and nutrition, activities to stimulate your mind and body, a safe neighborhood and home, and hope for the future. Given the changes that we already see underway in 1998, we must also add a new type of equipment—access to technology, information, and knowledge tools.

A sense of citizenship

We also want to challenge each of you to be an active citizen and good neighbor. Our group explored strategies for instilling these habits. Millions of young people help their communities as volunteers, and we think this is a good idea that will broaden your horizons as well as contribute to your neighbors' well-being. We also want to encourage you to gain practical experience in civics—dealing with community issues, expressing your opinions, taking part in decision making, and following through with problem-solving actions. As you mature, the responsibility for citizenship and neighborliness will fall upon your shoulders, and we want you to be prepared.

Economics

The history of economics in the United States demonstrates that there are periodically good times and bad times. In 1998, we certainly do not have a crystal ball that will predict the state of the economy in 2010, but we do guarantee that

- Well-developed competencies in reading, writing, oral communication, and math will be essential for your economic survival as a worker and consumer
- Completing a postsecondary education will increase the likelihood that you will earn a better income, and it will decrease the likelihood that you will experience poverty
- Lifelong learning will be an important habit—helping you bridge career and economic changes

- Skills in using knowledge and information technology will be an asset, and perhaps a necessity, in most occupations
- Abstinence from drug and alcohol abuse, tobacco, weapons, gangs, crime, and unsafe driving will increase the likelihood that you will survive long enough to earn a lifetime of income.

Values

Self-esteem, family, pride in your cultural roots, community service, hope, and faith all provide values that will serve as an anchor to your life. Even during your hard times and struggles, these will be resources that enable you to keep moving forward.

The news media

You will find it hard to believe, but a few of us older participants survived childhood without a television set! In contrast, most of you probably take television, cable and interactive computers for granted—like breathing or turning on a light switch.

Because television is such a big part of childhood and family life in 1998, our group spent time discussing the mass media, especially the potential of community-oriented journalism. We learned about news coverage and how some broadcast stations go out of their way to include "good news" about the accomplishments of children and youth. We felt this was particularly important because in 1998 we have seen a wave of "negative news" about children involved with handguns. (By 2010, have we finally outlawed easy access to handguns by children?)

We learned that the media can be a powerful resource for social change and community problem solving. One of the main pointers we learned, however, is that anybody who wants to gain media exposure must be persistent–reporters, editors, anchors, and news managers are busy people, and there is a lot of competition for media time. However persistence and sometimes even being "a pain in the butt" may eventually bring your issue into focus. Our group learned that "children's issues" have become a big deal in recent years. During the late 1990s, voters and politicians are talking a lot about children, education, and the schools. Our group hopes that everyone will make positive, concrete changes on your behalf—in addition to all the talk. We plan to work vigorously with the other people in an attempt to make it so.

Social change

As we have already suggested in this letter, participants in our meetings hope to accomplish much more than simply write a letter to you. We hope to take action and change society for the better—much as progressive Americans before us have done. Therefore, our meetings have included a discussion of recent movements in the United States. We have studied the environmental, antismoking, and anti-drunk driving movements in some detail.

We already have many of the elements of a movement to improve your future, and quite a few organizations and leaders are working toward that end. Before we can have a major impact, however, there are a number of issues that we must address:

- Many of us have a very specific age focus, such as preschool children, teenagers, etc. Until we figure out how to work together, it has often been difficult to address your overall development cycle—from prenatal through postsecondary education and entry into worklife.
- Professionals and researchers don't always stay in touch with parents, and vice-versa.
- Many efforts are compartmentalized by program or professional discipline—early childhood, elementary education, social work, health, public program, private program, etc.
- Groups promoting change and justice on behalf of specific racial and ethnic groups have not always had the time or interest to form alliances.

We hope that our meetings will be one of the early steps needed to bring everyone together in common pursuit of a better future for you.

Your responsibility

Even caring parents and other concerned adults cannot create a problem-free America. As always, there will also be plenty of problems remaining for you to solve, but we hope they won't be the same ones with which we are wrestling in 1998!

Best wishes for your future,

Children of 2010 Participants of 1998

Dialoging about the letter to the children of 2010

1. What would you add or omit from this letter?
2. Can you outline a letter of your own?
3. Consider writing your own letter to the Children of 2010

The Future

I pledge allegiance to the flag
of the United States of America,
and to the Republic for which it stands—
One nation under God, indivisible,
with liberty and justice for all.

Hundreds of thousands of school children recite these words as they begin each school day. In their words lie our common hopes and aspirations.

However, in the wake of demographic change, can we assume one nation *indivisible?* This is a question that we as a society cannot afford to leave unanswered, for how we today prepare for the future will define how well—and whether—democracy will work for the children of 2010. Previous generations have acknowledged their responsibility to the future, grappled with the need for change, and caused U.S. democracy to be an evolution that periodically reinvents itself. Now it is our turn.

Through the dialogue sessions and this book, we have gained a broadened awareness of the increasing demographic diversity and the daunting challenge of providing access to opportunity for all children. We have acknowledged that our commitment to one nation and a vibrant democracy mandates change. We have reflected on the urgency of taking action: We must make certain that every child has the necessary nurturing and preparation to participate fully in the social, economic, and cultural life of the United States.

In a democracy, such a vision requires improving the quality of life for all of our children: Not some of our children; all of our children. It means giving each child fair access to respect, a safe and nurturing environment, and doors of opportunity that span from prebirth to young adulthood. Improving each child's *quality* of life means our society must ensure that competent basic services and opportunities are available and accessible to all children. By "competent basic services," we mean that every child—regardless of cultural or individual differences—deserves the quality of health care, education, life experiences, and access to careers that you want for your own children.

In judging what our society needs to change, we recommend a very simple criterion: Would the quality of this service or opportunity or living environment be good enough for my own children . . . or for me, if I were a child again and faced with growing up in the 21st century?

As a conclusion to this book, we wish to challenge readers with a brief discussion of six questions: To make full participation in democracy accessible to all children of 2010, what changes must *you and I* make in our (1) lives, (2) professions and workplaces, (3) communities, (4) values, (5) the socioeconomic system, and (6) commitment to activism? Please note the *you and I,* because, in a democracy, there is no "them."

Our lives

Perhaps the greatest challenge of our generation is to be role models for the children of 2010 by demonstrating through our actions as well as words that an inclusive democracy is viable in our communities, workplaces, and nation. This will often require that we grow by reaching out beyond our own social enclave to listen, talk with, and cooperate with people who are different. The purpose of such interaction is not only dialogue or mutual understanding: In a democracy, we are called upon to share, to learn, and—yes—to engage in heated, constructive debate as a means for hammering out broad areas of consensus on which a majority of the U.S. population can agree.

We must demonstrate to our children and their children that we have the self confidence to share power and opportunity with citizens who are different, who at times march to the drummer of different needs and priorities. Sharing power is no easy task, either for groups who have enjoyed the privilege of power in the past or for those who aspire to it. Yet, the fire to broaden power and opportunity has historically heated the caldron in which U.S. democracy has brewed—property owners and tenants, industrialists and farmers, free and former slaves, men and women, investors and laborers, the privileged and the disenfranchised.

The 21st century asks us to take the next step in the evolution of democracy—one in which no single group will dominate our society. This is a logical step; a necessary step. In our everyday lives as citizens and neighbors, we need to show the children of 2010 how it works.

Professions and workplaces

An Anglo culture and population has been the historic context in which most professions in the United States have formulated their assumptions and defined their practices. Some of these paradigms will no longer be appropriate for the children of 2010, and each profession needs to take stock of itself—in explorations that are inclusive of the country's diverse population. Unfortunately, inclusiveness is difficult for many professions where numerous population groups may be severely underrepresented, and the only appropriate remedies will be to reach out to diverse persons who are outside of the profession—and to commence with initiatives to recruit and prepare a more representative group of practitioners within their profession for the future.

There are more dimensions to improving assumptions and practices of the professions than embracing a multicultural population, however. Many

community institutions, for example, have applied a "one size fits all" approach to education and other services that has often failed to recognize or respond to the individual differences of even the Anglo population. Many children from all racial and ethnic groups are unable or unprepared to run the gauntlet that has been put before them—as evidenced by underachievement, dropouts, teenage problems, and difficulty in making the transition to postsecondary education or the world of work. Addressing these problems, respecting individual differences, and introducing appropriate flexibility can benefit all children. Indeed, the theme of respect for and development of the individual potential of each child may be a unifying force around which all parents and families can solidify, in the 21st century, to pursue one nation indivisible.

We must also apply these ideas in our own workplace. This encompasses our relationship with colleagues, parents, children, customers, and the general public. We must take time to listen and observe instead of hastily pigeonholing individuals into categories or making unfounded assumptions about their potential contributions or resources. This demands time and energy, because it is far easier to throw people into the bins of worn-out stereotypes. It demands learning, and we will often be challenged to change our knowledge base and behavior.

Beyond individual change, we must also address institutional change in the workplace. If institutional policies and practices are limiting access to opportunity for some children and their families—or to our colleagues—we cannot afford to be silent. Let it be our generation that achieves needed change so the problems will not persist as millstones around the necks of the next generation.

Communities

Democracy is not possible unless all of us are connected as a community. This requires contact, communication, dialogue, and a means for accommodation. In a society where much of the adult population seems exhausted from long workweeks, commutes, and other responsibilities, realizing a sense of community is no trivial goal.

How to achieve a sense of community requires further exploration and discussion. Different cultures have divergent expectations about how and when to participate. The increase in nontraditional work hours also makes it difficult for many parents and other adults to assemble for meetings at set times. The question of when and how to involve teenagers and children in "community" also awaits further attention.

Technology may ultimately provide new options, as interactive and easy-to-use media (such as interactive television) become available. But achieving access to such technology may require much of the next decade before it is universally accessible to all of the population. Even then, accommodating language and other differences will require a new vision for a democratic medium. How to create universal access to such a community-building medium is a topic worthy of further discussion as we prepare for 2010.

Irrespective of technology options, democracy calls us all to be active participants. We as adults must demonstrate to the children that it is worthwhile to vote, go to meetings, voice our opinions, learn from the viewpoints of others, and serve as volunteers who meet community needs. We must give all children opportunities to participate as citizens—as volunteers, voices to be heard and respected, and participants in decisions that affect their lives.

Moreover, we must give children experience in establishing and maintaining broad communities with people who are different. It isn't enough for them to participate in their narrow neighborhoods or ethnic enclaves. The children of 2010 must be experienced in communicating, sharing power, and making joint decisions with children who are different, for a population with no dominating group is the context in which they must realize the dream of one nation indivisible.

Values

Why is it that television programming is dominated by so much violence, sex, and tawdry talk shows? It isn't millions of *them* watching the programming; it's we ourselves. In the process, we are communicating a wasteland of values to our children.

On our television screens, we're telling our children that it's OK to be entertained by watching people hurt and kill each other. That it's important to have a perfect body because people won't like you otherwise. That it's OK to treat other people as objects for sex. That it's important to have the latest clothing fashions and an expensive car (without explaining where the money comes from). Our radios spew similar messages, and our magazines promote no-holds-barred consumerism.

The children of 2010 will be smart enough to detect our hypocrisy. Unless we clean up our act, quickly, our generation will bequeath values that are counterproductive to a sense of community, democracy, and quality in interpersonal relationships.

Considerable discussion in recent years has focused on children's programming, but many children and youth also watch adult programming. The question then becomes, what do *we* do to demand that the media clean up *our* programming? What do *we* do to kick the habit of junk so that we can be role models for the next generation?

Of course, media programming is only the tip of the iceberg. Children learn from what we do in our own lives. Are family and other people really more important to us than career advancement or a new car? Is learning as important as entertainment in our lives? Is volunteering and sharing a part of our lifestyle? Is being open to other people and cultures part of our personal life?

Views about morality will differ, but a democratic society must place a high value on the quality of interpersonal relationships, respect for other individuals, and a sense of community.

Socioeconomic system

The fate of the children of 2010 rides in part on the wellbeing of their parents and families. Without change, a disturbing portion of future parents and their children will grapple with low incomes that blunt access to educational and other opportunities. William O'Hare and Joseph Schwartz write that "During the late 1960s, a person working full-time and year-round at minimum wage earned an income above the poverty line for a three-person family. By 1995, someone working full-time all year at minimum wage brought in an income 30 percent below the three-person poverty line." O'Hare and Schwartz observe that the children of "working poor" parents start out life with many disadvantages, and they are likely to repeat their parents' struggle with poverty "unless something intervenes to change the trajectory."[37]

At the first dialogue session, Harry Pachon noted forecasts of the bifurcation of the labor force into two broad groups—knowledge work and the service industry, with a split of approximately 20% of the workforce in the former and 80% in the latter.[38] Many of the service jobs are likely to offer low incomes to future parents and youth. A better future for the children of 2010 needs to be economically as well as culturally inclusive.

Economic inclusiveness might also alleviate tension about related matters, such as the debate regarding affirmative action. The unifying issue may be that we need to work together to create more opportunities for all children, rather than fight among ourselves over who gets scarce opportunities.

Commitment to activism

Each of us makes a difference when we work for specific results, know what we want to achieve, and can envision what a successful 21st century democracy looks like. Therefore, we challenge everyone to develop a vision of the future, broaden that vision through dialogue with others, search for answers to the questions raised by this book, and work together to realize our national ideal of one nation indivisible.

During the dialogue sessions, we explored movements that have changed the United States at the national, community, and individual levels. In each case, change required involvement, commitment, and sustained effort. The cause of democracy for the next generation of children demands nothing less.

The journey to 2010 begins with our involvement and commitment—yours and mine. We have every reason to hope that our efforts will lead to the further evolution of U.S. democracy, one in which our society can provide fair access to opportunity for all children, one that progresses toward the goal of one nation indivisible. Such a vision cannot be left to chance; it requires our personal involvement and ongoing activism.

This book frames issues and presents questions. As a democracy, we must work together, all of us, to devise answers and bring about needed change. The children of 2010 deserve nothing less.

Endnotes

1. M. Fix and J.S. Prassel. *Immigration and Immigrants: Setting the Record Straight.* Urban Institute, Washington, DC, 1994.

2. Harold L. Hodgkinson, based on presentation at April dialogue session. His recent studies include *The Same Client: The Demographics of Service and Delivery Systems* (1989); *All One System: Demographics of Education, Kindergarten Through Graduate School* (1989); *Higher Education, 1990-2010: A Demographic View* (1991); *The Demographics of American Indians: One Percent of the Population, Fifty Percent of the Diversity* (1992); *A Demographic Look at Tomorrow* (1992); *Immigration to America: The Asian Experience* (1994); *Hispanic Americans: A Look Back, A Look Ahead* (1995); *Bringing Tomorrow into Focus* (1996). All are available from the Institute for Educational Leadership, Washington, DC.

3. Edward N. Wolff. *The Rich Get Richer: Latest Data on Household Wealth During the 1980s.* Economic Policy Institute, Washington, DC. See also Edward N. Wolff, *Top Heavy: The Increasing Inequality of Wealth in America and What Can Be Done About It.* ISBN 1565843479. New Press, 1996. For reports that counter with recent economic gains for low income people, see "Poverty Rate Down, Household Income Up—Both Return to 1989 Pre-Recession Levels, Census Bureau Reports" at the Census Bureau web site, http://www.census.gov/hhes/www/income97.html and http://www.census.gov/hhes/www/povty97.html.

4. Mark Zepezauer and Arthur Naiman, *Take the Rich Off Welfare (Real Story Series).* ISBN 1878825313. Odonian Press, 1996.

5. "The New Face of America," *Time Magazine* Special Issue, Fall 1993.

6. Marvin R. Weisbord, *Discovering Common Ground: How Future Search Conferences Bring People Together to Achieve Breakthrough.* ISBN 1881052087. Berrett-Koehler, 1993.

7. Paul Martin DuBois and Jonathan J. Hutson, *Bridging the Racial Divide: A Report on Interracial Dialogue in America.* ISBN 0-9661626-0-9. The Center for Living Democracy, Brattleboro, VT, 1997.

8. Peter M. Senge (Editor), Charlotte Roberts, Rick Ross, Bryan Smigh, Art Kleiner, *The Fifth Discipline Fieldbook.* ISBN 0385472560. Currency/Doubleday, 1994.

9. David Bohm, *Unfolding Meaning: A Weekend Dialogue with David Bohm.* ISBN 0415136385. Routledge, 1985; Reprint Edition (June 1996).

10.   Benjamin Barber, *Strong Democracy: Participatory Politics for a New Age*. ISBN 0520056167. University of California Press, Paperback Reprint, 1985.

11.   For a broader discussion about disparity of access to higher education, see Thomas Mortenson, *Equity in Higher Educational Opportunity for Women, Black, Hispanic, and Low Income Students*, 1991. Also Mortenson's article "Family Income Differences Influence Educational Opportunity Every Step Toward Bachelor's Degree," *Postsecondary Education Opportunity*, June 1994. Other data are available in *The Condition of Education 1998*. National Center for Education Statistics, Washington, DC 1998; see especially "Percentage of 1992 high school graduates qualified for admission to a 4-year institution by level of qualification and family income," page 19.

12.   *Statistical Abstract of the United States*, Washington, DC; 1997.

13.   Presented by Dr. Harold L. Hodgkinson at the April dialogue session. Unpublished document from archive, Teachers College, Columbia University, New York.

14.   "How America Ages Depends on Race," *American Demographics*, April 1996.

15.   *School Age Demographics*, The General Accounting Office, Washington, DC; August 1993.

16.   *Kids Count*, Casey Foundation, Baltimore; 1997.

17.   K. Alaimo, R. Briefel, E. Frongillo, C. Olson, "Food Insufficiency Exists in the United States: Results from the Third National Health and Nutrition Examination Survey," *American Journal of Public Health*, March, 1998; pp. 419-426.

18.   Edward Twitchell Hall, *The Silent Language*. ISBN 0313222770. Greenwood Publishing Group, 1979.

19.   *Churches and Church Membership in the United States*, 1990, Glenmary Research Center, Atlanta; 1992.

20.   Dr. Hodgkinson cited the writings by Shelby Steele. A recent book by Steele is *A Dream Deferred: The Second Betrayal of Black Freedom in America*. ISBN: 0060168234. Harpercollins, 1998.

21.   George Gallup, Jr. (ed), *The Gallup Poll: Public Opinion*, 1997. ISBN 0842025979. Scholarly Resources, April 1998.

22.   Gallup Annual Survey, 1998.

23.   Beth Berselli, "Daniel Snyder Finds His Niche," *The Washington Post* April 13, 1998, pages B10–11.

24. Donald M. Norris and M. C. Joelle Fignole Lofton. *Winning with Diversity*. ISBN 0-88034-093-2. American Society for Association Executives Foundation et al.; Washington, DC, 1995; page 3.

25. John Allen Paulos, *The Los Angeles Times*, July 12, 1998; Page M3.

26. Henry P. Pachon, president of the Thomas Rivera Policy Institute at Claremont, CA. Related information is in the book: Harry Pachon and Louis Desipio, *New Americans by Choice: Political Perspectives of Latino Immigrants*. Westview Press, Boulder, CO, 1994. Dr. Pachon and Ana Sol Gutierrez (Montgomery County MD Board of Education) are interviewed by National Public Radio, First Hour of *Latino Series II*, August 1997; available as Real Audio at http://cgi.realaudio.com/contentp/npr/ne7A05.html. See also Harry P. Pachon, *New Citizens Are the New Target*, http://www.azteca.net/aztec/immigrat/pachon.html (undated). Papers of related works by other scholars available at the Thomas Rivera Policy Institute web site, http://www.cgs.edu/inst/trc.html.

27. Intellectual Capital. *Victims of the New Economy: IC Interview with Robert Reich*. Accessed at www.intellectualcapital.com/issues/97/1218/icinterview.asp; December 18, 1997.

28. Paul Simon, *We Can Do Better: How to Save America's Future—An Open Letter to President Clinton*, 1994.

29. *One America in the 21st Century: Forging a New Future*. The Advisory Board to the President's Initiative on Race, Executive Office of the President, Washington, DC; September 1998.

30. *Changing America: Indicators of Social and Economic Well-Being by Race and Hispanic Origin*. The Council of Economic Advisors, Executive Office of the President, Washington, DC; September 1998.

31. Virginia A. Hodgkinson et al., *Volunteering and Giving Among American Teenagers 12 to 17 Years of Age*. The Independent Sector, Washington, DC; 1996. (Updated every two years.)

32. Barry Checkoway, *Young People Creating Community Change*. W. K. Kellogg Foundation, Battle Creek, 1996.

33. Lisbeth B. Schorr, "Citizens Escape Poverty to Reclaim 'American Dream,'"*The Los Angeles Times*, October 23, 1997.

34. American News Service is a project of the Center for Living Democracy, Brattleboro, VT.

35. George W. Albee, "Foreword," in *Prevention: The Critical Need* by Jack Pransky. Burrell Foundation, 1991

36.   Geoffrey Canada, *fist stick knife gun.* ISBN 0-8070-0422-7. Beacon Press, Boston, 1995. Mr. Canada's most recent book is *Reaching Up for Manhood: Transforming the Lives of Boys in America.* ISBN 0807023167. Beacon Press, Boston, 1998.

37.   William O'Hare and Joseph Schwartz, "One Step Forward, Two Steps Back," *American Demographics,* September 1997.

38.   Dr. Pachon referred to the writings of Robert B. Reich, former Secretary of Labor. One of Reich's books addressing the U.S. workforce in the context of a global economy is *The Work of Nations: Preparing Ourselves for 21st Century Capitalism.* ISBN 0679736158. Vintage Books, 1992. See also endnote 20.